Mindfulness for Children

D1417685

Mindfulness for Children

SIMPLE ACTIVITIES FOR PARENTS AND CHILDREN TO CREATE GREATER FOCUS, RESILIENCE, AND JOY

SARAH RUDELL BEACH

CICO BOOKS
LONDON NEW YORK

To the teachers who have welcomed me into their classrooms, and to the parents who have welcomed me into their homes, to teach mindfulness to young people.

Published in 2020 by CICO Books
An imprint of Ryland Peters & Small Ltd

20–21 Jockey's Fields   341 E 116th St
London WC1R 4BW   New York, NY 10029

www.rylandpeters.com

10 9 8 7 6 5 4 3 2 1

Text © Sarah Rudell Beach 2020
Design and illustration © CICO Books 2020

Editor: Dawn Bates
Illustrator: Rosie Scott
Commissioning editor: Kristine Pidkameny
Art director: Sally Powell
Production manager: Gordana Simakovic
Publishing manager: Penny Craig
Publisher: Cindy Richards

The author's moral rights have been asserted. All rights reserved. No part of this publication may be reproduced, stored in a retrieval system, or transmitted in any form or by any means, electronic, mechanical, photocopying, or otherwise, without the prior permission of the publisher.

A CIP catalog record for this book is available from the Library of Congress and the British Library.

ISBN: 9 781 78249 606 9

Printed in China

CONTENTS

INTRODUCTION

What is mindfulness and why do we and our children need it?

When I first started writing online about mindfulness for children, one of the searches that brought someone to my blog was "how to teach mindfulness to an infant."

I smiled the moment I saw it.

For it really could be said that it is infants who teach us to be mindful. Our children come to us with no preconceptions, and an amazing capacity to be awed by the world around them. They are fully present, attuned to their surroundings, and insatiably curious about everything they encounter.

As we get bigger and busier, we tend to lose this natural presence in a flurry of activities and assignments and chores and grocery lists. We complain about our stressful and overscheduled days. We lament our inability to focus on our work, let alone on the things that "really matter." We see how distracted our children are, with social media and video games and sports and friends all competing for their attention. Many people are turning to the practice of mindfulness because they feel so stressed out by the demands of 21st-century life–they are trying to find some deeply needed moments of focus and stillness and quiet.

Mindfulness is our inherent ability to pay attention, with genuine curiosity and an attitude of allowing the present moment to be just as it is. We can pay attention to our internal experience (thoughts, emotions, bodily sensations) as well as our external surroundings: the sights and sounds in our environment and the tasks in which we engage. When we are present in this way, we can meet challenges with greater clarity and flexibility. We can experience joy as we savor the goodness around us, and we can cultivate resilience as we learn to be patient with unpleasant emotions or difficult experiences that may arise. Mindfulness helps us focus our scattered attention and soothe our frazzled nervous systems.

You might find it reassuring to know that the practice of mindfulness dates back over 2,500 years! Having a human brain and a human body means having a wandering brain and a vulnerable body. Life has always been hard… and philosophers and religious leaders have spent the last few millennia developing mind-body practices that can help humans find a bit of peace and stability in a chaotic world. Fortunately, 21st-century science is beginning to validate what

these philosophers and gurus have told us for 2,000 years: we can find peace and stability in the present moment. And we can help our children learn these valuable life skills as we prepare them for their joyful adult lives.

A GIFT TO OUR CHILDREN

There's a good reason why so many schools across the United States, Australia, and the United Kingdom have begun adopting mindfulness programs.

Teaching mindfulness to our children is a powerful gift. We can teach them how to recognize and manage their emotions, how to calm down when they are upset, how to focus on important tasks, and how to interact with others with empathy and generosity. These are fundamental skills that our children will need throughout their life, but we often don't teach them explicitly. We sometimes assume that they already know how to do these things. In fact, think of how often we demand that children "pay attention!" or "calm down!", without ever having taught them how to do so.

As parents, we can nourish and expand upon our young children's capacity for presence and engagement, and we can help our older children slow down and take a break from the daily stimulation of school and screens and sports and socializing that can lead to significant stress. We can teach them tools for enhancing their focus and concentration, for turning toward their difficulties without being overwhelmed by them, and for responding to challenges with skillful choices, instead of their habitual reactions.

MINDFULNESS IN ACTION

Imagine two siblings arguing about tidying their toys. It is loud and tense as they begin shouting over each other. The seven-year-old threatens to tell all about the five-year-old's transgressions, but as his frustration intensifies, he begins to notice his body is tense. He realizes how fast his heart is beating, and he discovers that his hands are tightly balled into fists. His forehead and jaw have become small and clenched. He notices the thought, "I'm always the one picking up the toys." Since he's been learning mindfulness in school, he remembers that these physical sensations and thoughts are signs that he is really angry, and he takes a moment to say to himself, "This is anger. I'm feeling really mad right now."

Acknowledging his anger, the seven-year-old takes a deep breath, feeling the air come in his nose and fill his lungs. As he breathes out, he tries to relax his body. He realizes he feels better when he does this, so he takes another deep breath. As he starts to relax, he notices the angry and scared look on his sister's face. His sister, who hasn't learned mindfulness yet, continues to yell. Her body is getting tighter, her voice louder, and her rage swells. She is angry and frustrated, but she isn't really aware of those feelings. There's just a lot of energy and movement in her body, and her arm begins to wind up as she prepares to strike her brother.

In my work teaching mindfulness to children, one of the most common stories I hear is how mindfulness changes how kids interact with their siblings. How they've noticed how angry they've gotten, and instead of lashing out or hitting, they take a moment and go to their room and breathe.

In the scenario above, the seven-year-old demonstrates many mindfulness skills: the capacity to pause and notice what's happening, an awareness of bodily sensations and thoughts, the ability to identify an emotion, the skill of breathing in a way that allows him to calm himself down, and the attention necessary to cultivate empathy and consider how his sister might be feeling at that moment.

His sister, meanwhile, knows she's not supposed to hit and yell and fight, but the feelings and sensations of anger and frustration overwhelm her little body. As the argument proceeds, fear mixes in with her other emotions, and, without prior practice in attending to her body and feelings and deliberately trying to calm herself down, she prepares to react with her fight-or-flight system engaged.

THE BENEFITS OF MINDFULNESS

A growing body of research indicates many benefits of mindfulness for kids, including:

• Improved focus and concentration

• Decreased stress and anxiety

• Improved ability to regulate impulses and handle difficult emotions

• Improvement in executive functioning skills (planning, decision-making, reasoning)

• Increased empathy and self-compassion

• A greater sense of calm

BECOMING JOYFUL AND RESILIENT

Mindfulness doesn't only help your children with everyday challenges as they are growing up. Being mindful becomes a way of being that benefits them their whole life, by making them joyful and resilient.

• When they are happy, they will be fully present with their joy, instead of clinging to it and hoping that things will never change.

• They will embrace the totality of their life experiences with curiosity, compassion, and wonder.

• They will discover what their challenges can teach them, and rejoice in their successes.

• They may not be happy all the time, but when they do encounter difficulties or setbacks, they will have the tools to handle them.

• They can be sad or angry or jealous or afraid or embarrassed or disappointed, without being overwhelmed by their experience.

• They will learn to turn toward their unpleasant emotions and determine what they need to do to take care of themselves.

• They will meet adversity with strength.

Joy is different from happiness. Happiness is fleeting and intense. It's a wonderful feeling, but not one that we can sustain indefinitely. We certainly can't be happy all the time; in fact, if we made our children's happiness our sole aim in parenting, we'd be setting up ourselves—and our children—for a lot of disappointment. Joy is deep and enduring. In Jennifer Senior's book about parenting, *All Joy and No Fun*, she boils down the difference between happiness and joy succinctly: "Joy is about being warm, not hot."

Happiness is often dependent on circumstances being a particular way, while joy can be the warmheartedness with which we meet all of our experiences.

As the happiness researchers tell us, the happiness we should be pursuing is not a perpetual smiley face, but what the Greeks called Eudaimonia. In his book *Stumbling on Happiness*, Daniel Gilbert translates this as "good spirit... human flourishing... [and] life well lived."

YES! That's what we want for our children. We want them to flourish, to live a good life in good spirits.

And our children can engage in their lives in this way if they are resilient. Resilience is the ability to handle a challenge without being overwhelmed by it. It's the ability to get back up when they've been knocked down. It doesn't mean that the difficulties aren't devastating or even traumatic. It means our children have the tools they need to recover. It means they know that they already possess all the skills they need to thrive.

REGULATING A BODY AND BUILDING A MIND

So now that we've got that out of the way... how do we actually DO that? How do we raise joyful, loving, and resilient children?

Let me first reassure you that you are doing a lot of it already! Every time you offer loving attention and encouragement to your children, you are strengthening their joy and resilience muscles. Any time you talk to your children about their feelings, offer a warm and soothing hug, listen to their jokes, kiss a skinned knee, or simply chat about their day at school, you are helping to wire their brain and regulate their nervous system in ways that promote flourishing.

There are lots of important things we need to do to care for our children. If we want to make things really simple, though, the two most crucial ways we support our children are by teaching them how to regulate their nervous system, and by assisting them in developing the cognitive and attentional skills necessary for successfully navigating the world. The beauty of mindfulness is that it provides a set of skills that support an embodied sense of calm and safety, and techniques for improving focus and working with a distracted mind.

When our children are born, their nervous systems are immature and they are unable to soothe themselves. We immediately begin to cuddle and comfort them, assisting them in calming their undeveloped nervous system. Within a few months, we're introducing them to the world of words and sounds and songs and ideas, all the while supporting their brain as it begins to wire itself for connection and comprehension. In these first few years, our supportive presence and engagement are already doing the powerful work of helping our child's nervous system become regulated and their brain become more integrated.

As our child enters the preschool and school-age years, we can begin to introduce them to simple and fun mindfulness practices that build upon the solid foundation of trust and safety we have already provided. The mindfulness exercises that you will learn in this book will support your child in these two important areas.

Regulating the body and nervous system: These skills include the ability to…

• Self-soothe

• Experience calm and relaxed states, and enter them when needed

• Recognize emotions as they arise

• Tolerate uncomfortable emotions

Building a mind: These skills include the ability to:

• Pay attention to what is important

• Ignore distractions and shift attention when necessary

• Understand other's feelings and ideas

With this foundation for self-regulation and attention in place, we can then teach our children important lessons about empathy, compassion, gratitude, communication, and service. We can support them in developing the qualities that the research tells us lead to joyful and resilient lives.

HOW TO USE THIS BOOK

In this book, you will learn fun and simple mindfulness activities that you can do with your children to help them build these essential life-long skills that promote focus, resilience, and joy. Start with Chapter 1 to learn the basics for yourself, and then you can explore the rest of the book and see which activities and skills might be most beneficial for your child. You can record notes in the log on pages 122–123 to keep track of the activities that seem to work best for your child.

In each chapter, you'll learn a bit more about the important emotional, cognitive, and social skills that you can support your child in developing. You'll then find several activities that you can engage in with your child to promote this skill, as well as additional opportunities to explore mindfulness.

Chapter 1: YOU

Discover how to become more mindful yourself. It's only by doing so that you can teach mindfulness techniques to your child.

Chapter 2: SOOTHE

Practice simple relaxation techniques with your child to help him discover a bodily sense of calm and safety.

Chapter 3: FOCUS

Learn a variety of mindfulness practices that support focus and concentration, such as mindful listening, mindful breathing, mindful seeing, and handling distractions.

Chapter 4: FEEL

Help your child understand his emotions by paying attention to his body and learning how his feelings actually *feel*. You'll also find strategies for working with difficult emotions without becoming overwhelmed.

Chapter 5: PAUSE

Once your child can identify her feelings and calm herself down, she needs to be able to make a wise choice. Discover strategies for investigating thoughts and stories, and seeing situations clearly before taking action.

Chapter 6: APPRECIATE

Learn how to savor positive emotions and nurture joy and happiness through practices like gratitude, mindful eating, and being mindful of boredom.

Chapter 7: CONNECT

Discover how mindfulness can help strengthen empathy, improve our communication with others, and connect to our larger community.

THE PATH OF MINDFULNESS

PARENT

Develop a mindfulness practice

Be the stable nervous system that helps to soothe your child

Model mindfulness practices for your child

CHILD

Find relaxation and ease in their body

Learn skills for paying attention and emotional regulation

Learn skills for pausing and making skillful choices

COMMUNITY

Develop empathy and compassion

Learn skills for navigating relationships and communicating with others

Learn skills for living with gratitude and joy

IN THE MOMENT

Most of the activities have an "in the moment" section, which explains how you can adapt the technique during your child's most stressful moments. Of course, mindfulness won't work if we only practice it during difficult moments.

AGE RANGES

Some of the activities include variations for younger children (ages 3–6) and older children (ages 7–11), but please recognize that these are just guidelines as all children differ in their development. Your 4-year-old may be ready to jump into an activity I've suggested for older children, or your 11-year-old may enjoy a playful game I've recommended for the little ones!

And mindfulness doesn't stop at age 11; in fact, the skills outlined in this book will be critical to your child's successful navigation of the adolescent years, as school becomes more stressful and peer relationships more challenging. Perhaps introduce your teenager to the activities that might be relevant to them (such as the relaxation techniques in Chapter 2 or the "wise choices" activities in Chapter 5), and then allow them to practice them on their own. With all of these activities, our ultimate hope is that once we teach these skills to our children, they will be able to use them even when we are not around!

KNOW YOUR INTENTIONS

Take a moment to check in with your intentions for teaching mindfulness to your child. Are you hoping that this will make your child quiet, or that he will start to behave in a way that makes things easier for you? Mindfulness isn't about getting our children to behave in any particular way, or about getting our children to act in ways for which they are not developmentally ready.

We teach mindfulness in much the same way we practice mindfulness: without an attachment to outcomes. We offer our children activities and instructions that help them relate to their own experience in a new way, and we help them fill their toolbox of strategies for the times when they are overwhelmed or upset. We may see immediate improvement in our child's abilities for self-regulation, or it may take a while for our child to determine the practices and techniques that work best for him. Be patient and accept your child for who he is in this moment; the learning will happen on your child's unique schedule.

MAKE IT CONSISTENT

Mindfulness is not a "use in case of emergency" technique. It is a skill that we must practice during the times when we are not experiencing a lot of stress and overwhelm, so that when we do hit those difficult moments, we will know what to do. In the chapters that follow, you will find lots of activities to do with your child to teach him mindfulness. Do these practices when your child is calm and eager to engage with you. If your child is having a full-on tantrum, he's not in any condition to learn about mindful breathing; in fact, your attempts to teach mindfulness to him during that time will only add to his sensory overwhelm. Once you've done these activities with your child, you can then gently remind him to "use his mindfulness" (or develop your own codes and signals) when he's entering meltdown mode, and support him in using these new strategies to maintain his equilibrium.

MAKE IT AN INVITATION

It's important to make learning mindfulness an invitation that you extend to your child, not something you force on him. As much as you can, keep it playful, and if your child is not interested, don't push it. He may be ready to learn from you in a few hours or a few months; in the meantime, continue with your own practice.

MAKE IT FUN

Most of all, have fun! I invite you to see the activities in this book as lovely opportunities for connection with your child: to play, to learn, to laugh, and to understand each other a bit more deeply. Be fully present with your child and genuinely listen to him. That's the most important gift you can give.

But first, let's start with you…

CHAPTER 1

YOU *Mindfulness for Parents and Caregivers*

You may be eager to share mindfulness with your child and want to get started on the fun activities that follow, but I urge you not to skip this chapter. It is arguably the most important one in the entire book—first it helps you to fully understand the concept of mindfulness before you try to teach it to your child, then it shows *you* how to become more mindful.

It's so important to dip your toes into the mindfulness pool before you take your children in with you, and the most important way you will teach mindfulness to your child is to model it yourself. When you take a moment to pause before responding, when you tell your children how you're feeling, when you listen to them with compassionate attention, or when you share something you're grateful for with them, you're teaching them mindfulness. You're teaching them to pay attention to the world with kindness and curiosity.

It's difficult, however, because this is not how most of us approach our own lives. In fact, *we* need these skills for paying attention and understanding our emotions just as much as our children do! Our children will always pay far more attention to what we *do* than what we *say,* so while teaching them the activities in this book will be a helpful first step, they'll learn so much more when they see you practicing mindfulness with them and around them throughout the day.

Mindfulness is an important skill that can actually help you to be a better parent. Studies have found that when parents practice mindfulness—even if they don't teach it to their children—it strengthens their relationship with their child, and their child's behavior even improves! This doesn't mean you'll be perfect; in fact, the times when you make mistakes can be wonderful opportunities to demonstrate how you repair relationships and take responsibility for your own behavior.

BEING A MINDFUL PARENT

When we parent mindfully, we apply the skills we cultivate in mindfulness practice. So we pay attention, stay open and curious, check in with our emotions, pause before responding, and notice our thoughts and judgments. We are fully present in our interactions with our children, and we accept our children for who they are in each moment.

Paying attention may sound easy, but studies have shown that we spend up to 50 percent of our time *not* paying attention. Mindfulness gives us a set of tools for paying attention to the present moment. We pay attention with *curiosity*, with a real interest in what is happening, and recognize that we don't know how things are going to turn out. For example, you may find it easy to pay attention if your child is screaming for her blanket, but you may notice that you aren't paying attention with curiosity. You may be wishing she would be quiet, or tell yourself "She's just mad that her blanket is in the wash and I know this is going to happen again next week," when you don't know if any of those things are true. To pay attention with curiosity means wondering *why* your child is upset right now. What caused *this* tantrum? What can I do *right now* that might help soothe my child?

Mindfulness means we pay attention without judgment, or at least we notice our tendency to judge. During your child's tantrum, you may notice a thought like, "She's so sensitive" or "He's so demanding." Or you may turn the judgment on yourself: "I can't believe he's throwing another fit. I must be a pretty awful parent." As you've likely experienced, these judgments usually don't make the situation better. With mindfulness, you might gently notice these unhelpful thoughts, and then return to paying attention to what is actually happening: a child is screaming and needs your help. You can imagine how helpful this way of paying attention might be in our daily lives. We could be present and attentive to our work and our relationships, we could catch unskillful thoughts before they spiral out of control, and we could ultimately be less reactive and more effective in our responses to stressors. In short, we'd be a lot more joyful and resilient.

A 2018 study found that parents who practiced mindfulness for eight weeks reported fewer problems in their parenting, less reactivity with their child, a better relationship with their partner, and improved wellbeing in their child. And the more parents demonstrated mindful qualities in their parenting, the greater the improvements in their child's functioning. It concluded that children "benefit from their parents becoming more mindful in parenting." Other research found that parents who practice mindfulness report less stress and an improved capacity to regulate their own emotions. They encourage more autonomy in their children, and are more engaged with them.

BECOMING ATTUNED

When we cultivate being present with our children, we can attune to our child. Child development experts have long known that one of the most critical factors in a child's emotional health is a stable, healthy attachment to a caregiver who is attuned to her needs. Through this relationship a child learns a basic sense of trust, develops a positive self-concept, and cultivates the ability to self-regulate

When we are attuned to a child's needs, emotions, desires, and dreams, we can better meet their needs. With younger children in particular, this is crucial; if they don't have the language skills to communicate with us, we must learn to read their emotional and behavioral signals. And we can only do this if we are paying attention. When we practice mindfulness, we improve our ability to attend to ourself and our children. When we pay close attention to our own experience, our nervous system becomes like a barometer—we can sense how our children are feeling and what they need. Our nervous system also acts like a tuning fork—children can "borrow" our stable, relaxed nervous system to regulate their own.

MINDFULNESS IN ACTION

I learned just how important mindfulness can be for parents one morning when my daughter was about six. We'd been having a difficult start to the day, and then I did the unforgivable—I asked her to put her socks on so we could get out the door and get to school.

Apparently, that request was enough to set her off. She began yelling at me, throwing her socks to floor, and then she screamed, "You are the WORST mom in the world!"

If you've ever been the recipient of these angry words, you know how it feels. I felt angry, insulted, and exasperated. I needed to get to work, and now THIS? My mind immediately started spinning a story about how ungrateful my child was, about all the diapers I had changed over the years and all the nights I'd stayed up with her... and now I was the worst mom in the world? I could feel my rage simmering just beneath the surface: a pounding heart, shallow breaths, tensed shoulders, clenched teeth. I wanted to yell.

But I remembered my mindfulness practice. I took a deep breath. And another. I didn't know what I was going to do, but I didn't yell. I had gathered enough presence in that moment to recognize that yelling wouldn't be skillful, it wasn't going to help my relationship with my daughter, and, most importantly, it wasn't going to result in my daughter getting her socks on and us getting out the door on time. I took another deep breath.

And then my daughter looked at me and said, "Well, you're not the worst mom in the world. I'm just mad at you right now."

A-ha! I realized that my mindful pause had invited my daughter to take a pause of her own. She just needed a moment to hear her words land, to see my wordless reaction to them, and she made amends. All on her own.

I share this episode with you to remind you that, one, you're not the only one who's been called the worst parent in the world, and two, to demonstrate how powerful this practice is. The gift of stopping and pausing is probably the most powerful gift mindfulness offers us. And when we can pause during a difficult moment and choose our response, instead of reacting based on our habits and conditioning, we give that gift to our children, too. Our own practice is a model and an invitation for our child.

WHY A FORMAL PRACTICE IS IMPORTANT

I often get asked by parents, "Do I really NEED to actually sit down and meditate? Is it enough if I just do things mindfully during my day?" I am of the strong opinion that, if we want to be more mindful, we need a formal practice. It's GREAT if you can bring your mindful attention to the things you do throughout your day, but it's also hard to do that if you're not, well, practicing how to do that!

Each time we sit down and pay attention to our breath, we are strengthening the neural networks in our brain that are responsible for paying attention. We know that the brain constantly changes in response to our experiences (a phenomenon known as neuroplasticity), so each time we bring our wandering mind back to our object of attention, we've improved our capacity for paying attention.

Mindfulness is a bit like exercise this way—it gets a little bit easier each time we do it. We may not see the results right away, but gradually we'll notice that, well, we're noticing things more, and we're remembering to pause and check in with how we're feeling before we react to something.

WE PRACTICE WHEN IT'S EASY SO WE CAN DO IT WHEN IT'S HARD

I say this in every training session I lead. It's hard to pause and notice your thoughts when your toddler is having a four-alarm meltdown in the middle of the grocery store. It's hard to calm your frayed nerves when you're trying to finally enjoy a few quiet moments for yourself and your five-year-old pops out of bed for the thirty-second time .

But it's easy to sit for five minutes in the morning and notice your breath when the house is quiet. It's easy to notice your thoughts when you're not surrounded by the noise and demands of the world. It's easy to check in with your body when no one is pulling on your arm or jumping into your lap.

It's in these quiet moments of our day that deep wisdom and insight can emerge. You might notice the same thoughts keep coming back again and again and again... which is really helpful information. Just like a recurrent ache in the body is a signal that something needs attending to, a repetitive thought or worry is an invitation to explore something that might be bothering us or that needs a new solution.

It's in the quiet moments of your day that you can discover the mindfulness practices that work best for you. Then, when you hit the challenging moments of your day, you will remember, "Yes! When I breathe like this, I feel better."

If you're new to mindfulness, I encourage you to start with just five minutes a day. I personally think morning is a great time for practice, because it helps you start the day with an embodied sense of peace and quiet. You can move into the rest of the day knowing you've already done something just for YOU. But you can also practice during your lunch break, or on the train during your commute, or right before bed. I know some parents who practice in their car in the parking lot before they drive home from work, or while they're waiting in the school pick-up line. Find the time of day that's going to work for you, and then try to commit to an entire week of formal meditation practice at that time.

MINDFULNESS OF BREATHING

Mindfulness practices often begin with the breath, not because there's anything particularly magical about the breath, but because it's always available. If you are breathing, and you know that you are breathing, you are present!

When we practice mindfulness of breathing, we may actually find ourselves thinking about breathing. As best you can, try to focus on the actual physical sensations of the breath (rising, falling, warmth, coolness, fast, slow, etc.).

Read through the description of this practice first, and then spend about five minutes focusing on your breath. You could also read the instructions out loud and record it on your phone, and then listen to the recording to guide you through the practice.

MINDFUL BREATHING PRACTICE

Find a comfortable posture that you can hold for the next five minutes. If you are seated, check that your spine is straight, but not rigid (upright, not uptight!). As best you can, relax any tension you may notice in your neck… your shoulders… your back… and your face (especially around your eyes and your jaw).

Let your breath be easy and natural. There's no need to try to control your breathing, or to breathe in a particular way. Just allow your body to breathe in and out, as it does all day.

Notice your in-breath, and just notice what it feels like as you breathe in.

Notice your out-breath, and just notice what it feels like as you breathe out.

Take a few more breaths, just noticing the sensations in your body as you breathe…

Notice the breath at the nostrils, feeling air coming into the nose, and then perhaps noticing the sensation of air coming out over the lips as you exhale… Take a few breaths just noticing the breath in your nose…

Notice the breath in the chest, sensing the rise of the chest on the inhale, and the fall of the chest on the exhale … Take a few breaths, just noticing the breath in the chest …

Notice the breath in the belly, feeling how the belly expands as you breathe in, and how it softens as you breathe out … Take a few more breaths, just noticing the breath in the belly …

Notice your next in-breath in your entire body, imagining breathing from the bottom of your feet to the top of your head, filling your lungs and tissues with nourishing oxygen …

Notice the out-breath, imagining breathing out from the top of the head to the bottom of your feet, exhaling what your body no longer needs …

On the next breath in, breathe in whatever it is YOU need… perhaps patience, or compassion, or stillness …

As you exhale, imagine breathing out something you no longer need … perhaps resentment, or anger, or busy-ness …

Take a few more deep breaths, noticing how it feels in your body to have spent a few moments in relative quiet and stillness …

Before you open your eyes, take a moment to thank yourself for the gift of a few moments of self-care.

MINDFULNESS OF THE BODY

When we're worked up, the rational and thinking part of our brain has gone offline, and more primitive, defensive regions take over. Those parts don't speak English, or any other language. They speak the language of the body. So we soothe them by relaxing the body.

MINDFULNESS OF THE BODY PRACTICE

Check in with your body. Can you feel your feet? What do you notice? Are they warm, cold, tingling, itchy, or something else? Just notice the sensations ...

Can you feel your hands? Are they still or are they moving? Are they tense or relaxed? What do you notice?

Can you feel the surface you are sitting or standing on? Where does your body make contact with the ground or the chair? What does it feel like in those spaces? See if you can notice the gaps between your body and the chair ...

Gently scan your body and see what else you notice. Perhaps you notice tension ... or relaxation ... tightness ... or softness ... movement ... or stillness ... or any other sensations of pressure ... or buzzing ... or warmth or coolness ...

See if you can find a place in your body that feels pleasant, somewhere in the body where there is a sense of ease and relaxation ... perhaps in the hands, or in the movement of the breath ... If it's hard to find a pleasant sensation, see if you can find a place in the body that feels neutral ...

Spend a moment focusing your attention on this part of the body. Imagine this pleasant sensation in your body is an anchor for your attention, a place you return to if your attention wanders away. Notice if the mind wanders, and if it does, simply bring your attention back to this pleasant or neutral sensation ... Does anything in your experience change or shift when you place your attention here? (It's okay if you don't notice a change, too!)

Take a few deep breaths ... Notice how the body feels after spending some time paying attention to it ... Notice the thoughts or feelings that are present ... And when you are ready, you can open your eyes.

MINDFULNESS OF THOUGHTS

We have approximately 50–70,000 thoughts in a day and although we are often unaware of them, they color our experience nonetheless. For many of us, the constant narration in our heads is often negative, full of self-criticism, worry, regret, judgment, and exaggeration.

MINDFULNESS OF THOUGHTS PRACTICE

We are not trying to stop thinking (that would be impossible); we're simply becoming aware of our thought patterns. We're starting to notice both the helpful and unhelpful thoughts. And once we notice them, we can work with them more effectively, and not be completely driven by them.

Allow yourself to settle into a comfortable seated or lying down posture, closing your eyes and bringing your attention to your breath... As you allow your attention to settle on the breath, you'll likely notice thoughts pulling your attention away. When this happens, just silently say to yourself, "thinking, thinking." See what happens to the thought when you simply acknowledge it, and then return your attention to the breath. You don't have to try to stop the thought, or push it away. Just notice it.

If a thought is persistent, you can allow your attention to rest on the thought itself. Try to notice the qualities of the thought, instead of the actual content of the thought. Is this thought fast or slow? Loud or soft? Pleasant or unpleasant?

Perhaps you can imagine each thought as a cloud. Just as clouds pass through the sky, thoughts pass through your awareness. You can simply watch their movement, instead of controlling them. If you notice a particularly difficult or challenging thought, you can ask yourself: Is this thought true? Is this thought helpful? Is there a different thought that would be more helpful or accurate?

As best you can, see if you can bring your attention back to your breath each time you realize that you have been wrapped up in thought.

When you finish, it may be helpful to journal about the thoughts that arose.

MINDFULNESS FOR A STRESSFUL MOMENT

When you hit a stressful moment, combine all three of these mindfulness practices in a quick mindful minute.

1. Breathe: Take three deep breaths, noticing the physical sensations of each in-breath and each out-breath.

2. Sense: Notice the sensations in your body. Can you feel your feet? Your hands? What do you notice in the environment around you?

3. Think: What thoughts do you notice? Are you making up a story? Are you seeing the situation clearly? Are you judging or observing?

4. Respond: Act from a place of calm knowing.

CULTIVATING EMPATHY

One of the challenges of mindful parenting is that the times when our children most need our empathy and compassion are the times when their behaviors are least likely to evoke those feelings in us. This practice will help you cultivate greater empathy for and understanding of your child.

Close your eyes and take a few deep breaths…

Bring an image of your child to your mind. Picture her laughing or smiling or doing something she loves to do. See her at her happiest, at her best…

See if you can identify three things that are absolutely amazing about your child. What makes her awesome? Spend some time focusing on these great qualities of your child.

Next, think about some of the things that your child struggles with right now. What is hard for her? Why is this hard for her? See if you can put yourself in your child's position, perhaps even remembering yourself at this age and what you were like. What was hard for you when you were her age?

Notice if you're making any judgments about your child. It's okay if you are… the mind is constantly judging. If you do notice judgments, see if you can set them to the side and focus on your child's actual behavior and struggles. Is there a different way to interpret her difficulties?

Ask yourself, what does my child need from me? How can I support her? What does she need to learn so this isn't so hard for her? Can some of her great qualities help with this thing she is struggling with?

Take another deep breath, and place your hand on your heart. Imagine sending your child the help, the support, and the love she needs. You can even silently say to your child, "I know this is hard for you. I will do my best to support you and teach you. I love you."

Then open your eyes and notice how you feel.

This is a great practice to follow up with some journaling about the thoughts, feelings, and ideas that emerged.

CHAPTER 2

SOOTHE *Finding Relaxation and Ease*

From the moment your child was born, you began doing one of the most important tasks of mammalian parenting: you soothed him. The snuggling, swaddling, cooing, rocking, singing, smiling, bathing, and many other ways you gently engaged your child, helped him to soothe his own immature nervous system. You helped him understand what it feels like to be calm, relaxed, and at ease.

These soothing rhythms of infant care may feel instinctual because, in many ways, they are. As humans evolved, a dilemma emerged: if our brains got much bigger, so would the cranium that protected it, making it impossible for a baby to fit down the birth canal. As a result, humans evolved to be born quite immature compared to other mammalian infants, with a brain that still needed a lot of development, and therefore a nervous system that couldn't yet self-regulate.

Enter parents. As human infants are born helpless and unable to soothe themselves, they require the presence of attentive and well-regulated adults to help them experience a calm and stable state and be at ease. And yet, in our busy lives, we often impart to our children our own dysregulation and busy-ness and agitation.

As our children get older, their lives begin to reflect the chaos of our own, with school activities and sports and enrichment classes to fill the days, and lots of doing, instead of being.

As a result, our children not only don't know how to soothe themselves and calm down—they may not even know what calm feels like! I've come across this in my work with children. Once, after leading a guided relaxation activity for a group of kindergarten children, a young girl stood up and exclaimed, "Wow, I really needed that! I never let my body rest!"

One of the most powerful "side effects" of mindfulness is a feeling of calm. In this chapter, you will learn simple exercises to do with your children that will help them (and YOU!) reconnect to a feeling of rest and ease in their body. You'll spend time together in being mode, not doing mode. This ability to find stability and feel grounded and at ease is fundamental to all the other mindfulness practices that help us pay attention, understand our emotions, make good decisions, and interact skillfully with others.

BELLY BREATHING

Babies breathe with their entire body and a relaxed belly. It's amazing how quickly we lose this natural and primitive style of breathing and, instead, take shallow breaths from our chest that do not promote deep relaxation. This exercise is about getting back to our baby breath. Try practicing it with your child for a few moments each day.

TRY THIS TOGETHER

Do the following sequence with your child. It works well for all ages, but check out the variations opposite.

Lie alongside your child on the floor or on a bed and place your hands on top of your belly. Ask your child to place his hands on his belly too. Now, you can both just breathe naturally and see if you notice your hands moving up and down. If your breathing—or your child's breathing—is shallow (mainly in the chest), you may not notice much movement, and that's okay. The point is simply to bring your attention to your breath.

Next, try to engage your belly as you breathe. When you breathe in, imagine that your belly is a balloon, and you want to fill it as much as possible. (Sometimes children tense up when they are given this instruction, so encourage your child to let his arms and legs and whole body be loose.)

When you breathe out, imagine that you are squeezing all the air out of your belly. Let the balloon deflate as much as possible (it's hard to breathe more air into the balloon on the next breath if it's still full with the last breath). You can instruct older children to imagine that they are pulling their belly button down to the floor below them (this engages the diaphragm in helping to expel the air from the lungs).

Take a few more breaths this way. Now can your child notice his hands moving up and down with each breath? What does it feel like to breathe this way? Is it different from how he normally breathes?

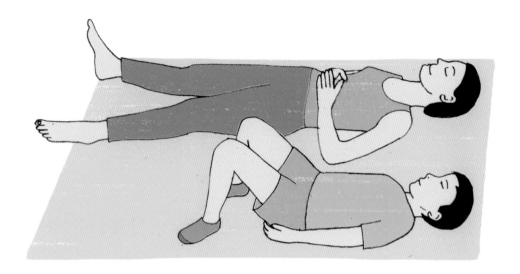

VARIATION FOR AGES 3-6

• Place a stuffed animal or toy on your young child's belly. Watching it move up and down creates a more helpful visual for him.

VARIATION FOR AGES 7-11

• Older children can try additional practices for deep breathing. Ask them to try 4-6 breathing, where they make their inhale last a full four counts, and their exhale last a full six counts, or resonant/coherent breathing, where each in-breath and out-breath is the same length, but the breathing is slower (five or six counts to inhale, five or six counts to exhale).

More to Explore

If your child has infant or toddler siblings or cousins, encourage him to watch them breathe, and notice how natural their breath is and how big their belly gets with each inhale. Though sometimes infants have a slightly faster respiration rate, you could both try to match the baby's breath (perhaps not the actual pace, but the style), and notice how it feels. Ask your child, "Why do you think we stop breathing this way as we get older?"

TENSION TAMER

Feeling calm and soothed is fundamentally a physical experience —
a sensation of being relaxed and safe. Sometimes it's easier to feel calm
when we contrast it with feeling tense. That's what this exercise,
which is suitable for children of all ages, is intended to demonstrate.

TRY THIS TOGETHER

Standing side-by-side with your child, both take a deep breath in and bring your arms up above your head. Then squeeze your hands into fists, and tighten your arm muscles. Then scrunch up your face, squeezing your eyes shut and tightening your mouth and wrinkling your nose. Then squeeze your chest, belly, legs, feet, toes… anywhere there's a muscle in your body that you can contract, contract it! Make your body as tight as possible…

And then release! Try it again (breathe in and make everything tight) and this time be really dramatic on the exhale as you un-tighten your body—allow your arms to flop to the side, make your exhale loud and forceful, and allow your legs to bend and bounce as you experience the release of tension from your body.

Invite your child to be playful—he can make silly noises with his out-breath, or stick his tongue out, or imagine he's a cooked noodle softening all the way to the floor as he relaxes.

Repeat as often as feels good!

More to Explore

Questions to ask your child:

• What did it feel like when your body was tight? Did it feel comfortable or uncomfortable? Do you think your body is sometimes tight like that without you even trying to make it tense?

• When you tightened your body, did it change your feelings? (Younger kids may not notice this, but older children might recognize that just feeling tense in their body can provoke feelings of anxiety or worry.)

• What did it feel like when you relaxed your body?

• What would it be like if we remembered to relax our body during the day?

• When you feel tense or worried, where do you think it shows up most in your body?

IN THE MOMENT

This is a great practice for intense moments when your child needs to be calmed down quickly. If you notice signs of him becoming agitated (pursed lips, a furrowed brow, tight shoulders, a stiff neck, or overall bodily rigidity), you can remind him of this exercise: "Oh, your body looks like it's getting tense. Let's go with it and tighten EVERYTHING in our body… and now whoosh! Let's let that tension out."

CALM DETECTIVE

For kids, and adults, it's a lot easier to calm down when we know the techniques that work best for us. In this practice, you'll help your child determine what is soothing and calming for him.

YOU WILL NEED

• Age-appropriate items that your child might find soothing, such as a favorite book, blanket, pillows, stuffed animal, warm beverage, gentle music, hairbrush, scented oil, lotion, a heating pad

• Paper and markers/crayons/pencils to record your investigations

• Old magazines for cutting up

• Scissors and glue

TRY THIS TOGETHER

Ask your child if he knows what "calm" means. He may struggle to put it into words. I like to define it as a sense of ease or relaxation; of being content with things exactly as they are and having what you need. There's a subtle sense of feeling comfortable in your body and completely safe. As appropriate for your child, you can share any of those definitions.

Ask your child when he feels calm—at ease, relaxed, content. What activities (or non-activities) help him to feel this way? It may help to ask him to recall a time when he felt calm. Closing his eyes might make it easier to bring this to mind. Once he has a picture of it in his mind, ask, "What does it feel like in your body? What do you notice in your face, shoulders, chest, belly, or legs?" If he is still struggling, ask him to think about how he feels before falling asleep, when his body is relaxed.

Now tell him that you are both going to be "Calm Detectives" to investigate what helps us to feel safe, relaxed, and soothed.

Show your child the items you have gathered and ask him to explore how each one makes him feel—for example, reading aloud from a book, snuggling a blanket, drinking warm cocoa. Encourage him to use all his senses—touch, smell, hearing, taste (if appropriate), and sight. With each one, take a deep breath and ask your child to notice what his body feels like. Remind him there are no right or wrong answers. An older child can write down or draw the results of his investigation (you could make a Detective Notebook).

Now ask your child to go on a scavenger hunt for other items that he finds soothing or calming. Talk about why he chose those items, and how he could use them when he feels upset.

IN THE MOMENT

Encourage your child to keep his Detective Notebook, Calm Treasure Box, or Calm Chart (see page 38) somewhere visible and easily accessible so you can direct him to it when he gets upset.

VARIATIONS FOR AGES 3-6

• Ask your child to draw a picture of himself doing something that is calming for him.

• Create a Calm Treasure Box with soothing items that your child can use when he's upset.

• Find an outline image of a child and ask your child to color in what calm feels like in his body (for example, his heart or tummy feels warm, or his head feels sleepy). He could use different colors to represent the feelings of warmth, relaxation, or rest in his body.

VARIATIONS FOR AGES 7-11

• Encourage your older child to find items for YOU to test to see how they feel. Talk about why your child chose those items.

• Find some magazines and ask your child to cut out images of things that he finds soothing and glue them onto a poster board as a visual reminder of the things that he can do to self-soothe. You could also create a Pinterest board or a digital vision board of soothing images and activities.

• Since calm is often defined by what it is NOT, you could have a conversation with your older child about what NOT feeling calm is like (which may be easier). Once he identifies a not-calm feeling, ask what the opposite of that would be. You could ask him to create a list or chart like this:

My Calm Chart

How NOT being calm feels

How being calm feels

What I can do to feel calm

More to Explore

• As a Calm Detective, your child could ask other family members or their friends what makes them feel calm. Talk with them about what they learned, and if there are any similar techniques they would like to try out!

• Create a "Calm Down Place" in your house where your child can go when he needs a moment to soothe himself. He can decorate it with anything he wants, and include the objects that he found most soothing. Consider using the Calm Down Place as an alternative to a "time out."

DEEP RELAXATION

This is a great practice to do before bedtime, especially if your child has trouble settling down at night or falling asleep.

TRY THIS TOGETHER

Once your child is settled in bed, read the instructions below. For a younger child, the practice should last about 5-10 minutes, depending on how he responds to it and how long he can pay attention to the practice. For an older child, you can pause a bit between the different sections.

Close your eyes and just allow yourself to rest… If you feel wiggly or really awake, that's okay. See if you can take a few deep breaths and notice if that helps your body relax a bit. Feel your breath coming in through your nose, and then notice the air rushing out when you breathe out.

You're going to imagine that you have a magic flashlight that you can use to relax your body. The light that shines out from this magic flashlight can be any color you want it to be, and is gentle, warm, and relaxing. See if you can imagine this flashlight…

This flashlight is so magical that you can make it move just with your mind. Right now, imagine that you are shining this flashlight on your feet. Your feet relax as the warm light shines on them. You can let your feet be loose and just rest completely on the bed. They've done lots of work for you today and this magic light is taking care of them and letting them go to sleep…

YOU WILL NEED

• The guided practice below to read to your child

• Blankets, pillows, or any other comfort items that might help your child relax

Now imagine shining the light of the flashlight on your legs… Imagine it's making your legs feel warm and relaxed. You did a lot of running and walking and standing today, and now it's time to let your legs rest. See if you can make your legs be as loose as spaghetti, completely relaxed…

Let this flashlight now come up to your belly, letting your stomach relax as you breathe in and out. Imagine the light coming up to your heart and filling it with warmth. Allow your belly and your chest to relax as this soothing light surrounds and protects you…

Now shine this soft light on your arms… See if you can let your arms be really heavy as they just sink into the bed. Your arms did a lot of work today, and now they can just rest…

Now the light gently moves up to your head, helping you relax the muscles of your face. You can let go of any worries or thoughts about your day and just let your mouth, nose, and eyes relax…

If there's anywhere else in your body that could use some warmth and light, shine your magic flashlight there and imagine that part of your body relaxing as the light continues to glow…

Just notice how your whole body feels right now, imagining that this magic light has now filled your entire body so you can feel rested and warm. You can dim your flashlight a bit as you get ready for sleep, or you can turn it off, knowing that whenever you need to relax your body, you can always bring it out again and shine some warmth and relaxation anywhere your body needs it.

If your child is quite sleepy and ready for bed after this practice, you can tuck him in for sleep. Alternatively, you could talk with him about what the Deep Relaxation exercise felt like.

VARIATIONS FOR AGES 3-6

• The biggest challenge for young children may be the length of this practice. Try to keep the first Deep Relaxation to under 5 minutes, focusing on just a few main areas of the body. You can gradually increase the time if your child enjoys it.

• You may need to be more specific about where in the body to direct your child's attention—for example, "notice your left foot," "shine the light on your right arm"—as younger children will benefit from more concrete instructions.

VARIATIONS FOR AGES 7-11

• If your older child finds the "magic flashlight" a bit silly, invite him to come up with his own idea for something that would allow him to pay attention to and soothe different parts of his body—perhaps a microscope, a magnifying glass, or something else.

• For each area of the body you focus on, instruct your child to take a moment to be thankful for all the things he used that part of his body for that day (e.g., legs for walking to school, arms for writing or doing art projects, brain for thinking, face for smiling and talking).

More to Explore

• As with any practice, Deep Relaxation may not always feel relaxing—and that's okay. Talk to your child about what he did notice, and where in his body he noticed it. If it didn't feel relaxing to your child, normalize that and ask him why it might have been hard. You could explain that sometimes our worries get so big they show up in our bodies, but it's really helpful to do something like this so we can notice them. Invite your child to talk to you about any worries or difficulties that may have made it hard for him to feel soothed.

• Conversation starters:
  What did it feel like to let your body completely relax?
  Where did your body feel most relaxed?
  What part of your body was hardest to relax?
  Is there another time during your day that you could imagine a magic spotlight shining on you to help you relax?
  {If this practice felt relaxing}: Do you ever feel this relaxed at other times of the day? What are you doing when you feel relaxed and soothed? Maybe we should do more of that activity!

IN THE MOMENT

If the magic flashlight is a helpful image for your child, you could use that phrase as a cue for him when you notice he is starting to get upset or agitated. You might say, "It looks like you're getting frustrated right now. Do you think you could take out your magic flashlight and see if that helps you relax a bit and then we can figure this out?"

MY SAFE PLACE

This practice draws on the power of your child's imagination to create a safe place in his mind that he can always turn to when he is overwhelmed, frightened, or anxious.

TRY THIS TOGETHER

Once your child is sitting or lying comfortably, ask him to close his eyes, then read this script:

Take a deep breath, and imagine that you are walking down a beautiful path. Maybe it's a path that you recognize [you could insert the name or description of a path your child may know], or maybe it's brand new to you. In your imagination, take a moment to look around at this path. What trees or flowers do you see? What can you hear? What does this place smell like? Is it winter or summer here?

Just up ahead, you can see a small turn in the path, so let's see where it leads. Imagine stepping onto this new part of the path, and after you take three more steps, you realize that you are in the most beautiful and relaxing place in the world. What is this place? Is it inside or outside? If it's outside, what is it like? Is it warm? Is it a garden or a beach or a park? If it's inside, what kind of room is it? Is it a bedroom or a living room?

Take a moment and stand in this place knowing that it is only for you. No one else knows where this special part of the path is. You are completely safe and protected here.

What can you see in your special place? What colors are around you?

What can you hear? Are there birds or gentle animals around you? Is it quiet?

What can you smell? If you are outside, can you smell flowers or grass? If you're inside, can you smell food cooking or a candle burning?

What does it feel like in this place? Is it warm? Is there sunlight or a heater? Or is there snow to play in?

After looking around and noticing your special place, you may realize something else needs to be here. It is your special place, so you can have anything you want. Take a moment to get the space perfect for you. Does it need a chair or a couch? A bed? A blanket? You get to make this space exactly as you want it to be!

If there's a place to sit or lie down in your special place, go ahead and let yourself rest here. Imagine yourself completely at ease and totally safe. What does it feel like to be here?

Now that you've had some time to get to know your safe place, get up and find your way back to the path. Take a moment to look at your special place, knowing that no one else will be able to find it, and when you come back, it will be just as you are leaving it. Take a few steps to return to the main path, and remind yourself that you can close your eyes and visit this safe and special place anytime you want to.

VARIATIONS FOR AGES 3-6

• Younger children may need more guidance to imagine their safe place. Offer just a few simple suggestions that will resonate with your child: a beach, a garden, a park, or a comfy room.

• Ask your child to draw a picture of his safe place first. Prompt him to think about a place he loves or what makes him feel safe, and to include as much detail as he is capable of.

• Find out if your child would like a special person or guide with him in his safe place— perhaps a parent, a teacher, or a good friend?

VARIATION FOR AGES 7-11

• Ask an older child to write about his safe place. Prompt him to think about a place he loves or what makes him feel safe, and to include as much detail as he is capable of. That way he will be able to bring it to mind more easily.

IN THE MOMENT

If your child draws his safe place, post it somewhere he can see it frequently. You could ask him to name it, so that when he is feeling overwhelmed you can gently say the name as a reminder.

CHAPTER 3

FOCUS *Learning to Pay Attention*

Mindfulness, fundamentally, is paying attention. After practicing the soothing activities in Chapter 2, your child has a strong foundation for cultivating her attention; once her body is relaxed, she has a stronger ability to direct her attention and observe what is happening in her mind.

Paying attention is one of the most important skills children (and adults) need in order to do well at school, or to do anything that requires focus and careful attending. We frequently implore children to "Pay attention", and assume they know how to, but we rarely teach them or provide them with the skills to do so more effectively.

Paying attention involves several different skills:

• Sustaining attention—focusing on the current task, and being able to persist in attending to it (for example, being able to focus on homework for the entire duration of the time needed to complete it).

• Shifting attention—being able to turn attention elsewhere when necessary (for example, being able to temporarily stop doing schoolwork and focus on a conversation with a teacher, and then return to the assignment).

• Ignoring distractions—being able to keep one's attention on a task even when irrelevant distractions are present (for example, focusing on homework while the sounds of preparing dinner are being made).

When you teach your child to pay attention, you help her to cultivate her curiosity and interest in the world. You will also help her to discover that her attention is a resource. She has a choice in what she pays attention to, and she can focus more intently on the things that are important to her or that make her feel joyful. She can also learn how to shift her attention from unpleasant thoughts and worries to more neutral objects like her breath or her immediate surroundings. Attention is powerful!

By doing the activities in this chapter your child will learn fun ways to practice paying attention. Any time your child attends to her breath or to the sounds around her, she is strengthening the neural networks in her brain that support focus and concentration.

MY MIND IN A JAR

Making "mind jars" is a fun craft and a great way to teach children about how mindfulness practice helps them calm down and focus.

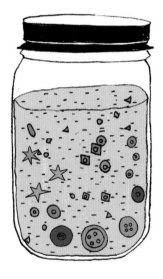

YOU WILL NEED

• A jar with a lid (a canning jar works well)

• Water

• Glitter or a glitter alternative (sand, sequins, microbeads)

TRY THIS TOGETHER

Add water to the jar until it is about three-quarters full. Invite your child to add as much glitter, or an alternative, to the jar. It's helpful to use something that will sink to the bottom—small beads or buttons work well. Have fun mixing different colors and textures (if you're using sand, you could add food coloring).

Tightly seal (or even glue) the lid onto the jar. Your child can decorate the top of the jar with permanent markers or other craft supplies as desired.

Explain to your child that the jar represents her mind that is often really busy with thoughts. (Shake the jar to show the swirl of beads, glitter, etc. to represent how our minds can get completely clouded with our thoughts or our strong feelings.) What does it feel like when this happens?

Then take a few moments to do some mindful breathing (see page 23) with your child. As you take deep breaths, watch how the contents of the jar settle to the bottom. Once they've settled, ask your child how she feels. (She may report feeling relaxed or calm, although any response is fine.) Then talk about what the mind jar looks like now (it's much calmer and the water is clear).

Explain how the same thing can happen with our mind. It might feel frenzied and busy, but if we stop for a moment, and let our body rest while we take a few deep breaths, things settle down and our mind gets a bit clearer.

IN THE MOMENT

If you have created a calm-down area in your home (see page 38), a mind jar is a great resource to keep there. When your child feels overwhelmed, she can sit with her jar and shake it up, and take several deep breaths while she watches the glitter settle.

VARIATION FOR AGES 3–6

• The concept of a "busy mind" may be difficult for younger children to grasp. It may be easier for them to understand busy-ness and over-activity in their body. Ask them to stand up and hold their mind jar with both hands as they twist their body side to side, jump up and down, or wiggle as fast as they can. Then set the mind jar down and ask them to notice how their body probably feels like the jar looks—all swirly and active and unsettled. Take a few deep breaths and notice what happens to the jar, their body, and even their thoughts during a few moments of rest.

VARIATION FOR AGES 7–11

• Ask your older child if she ever feels like there's just too much running through her head at school. She might feel overwhelmed trying to balance schoolwork, homework, friendships, and everything else she needs to attend to during the day. Tell her that she can try to visualize her mind jar even when she's at school. She can take a few deep breaths at her desk so everything can settle and she can see things a bit more clearly.

More to Explore

• Using a snow globe, if you have one, is also a good way to illustrate this concept without the mess of glitter!

• Some follow-up questions to ask your child after you make a mind jar might be: What happens when we try to make a decision when our mind is all busy and shaken up? How might our decision be different if we made it when our mind was clear and settled?

FIND YOUR ANCHOR

Like the exercises on pages 23 and 25, this one uses the concept of having an anchor to hold your attention in place. Just like an anchor keeps a boat from drifting away, paying attention to our breath keeps our mind from wandering. If children can identify a specific place in their body to notice their breath, it's a lot easier for them than being told to "breathe."

TRY THIS TOGETHER

Ask your child how often she is aware of her breathing. She'll probably reply that she notices her breath when she's been running fast, or if she's scared, or at some other time when her breath has sped up. Remind her that she's breathing all day long… but it's something she may not usually notice!

Ask your child to notice her breath right now, breathing in and out. Comment on how it can be a bit hard to focus on, even when we're trying to notice it, because the breath can be so quiet! Explain that you're going to explore with her the different places in our body where we can notice our breath, and see if that helps.

Ask your child to place her hand under her nose. Can she feel the warm air on her hand as she breathes out? Can she really notice the breath as it enters her nose, fills her nostrils, and then leaves her nose? Suggest that she places the back of her hand in front of her mouth as she exhales. Can she feel the warm air on her hand?

Ask your child to place her hands over her chest. Can she feel how her chest moves up and down as she breathes? What happens when she takes a really deep breath?

Ask your child to place her hands on her stomach. Can she feel her belly get big and full when she breathes in? Can she feel it soften and get smaller when she breathes out?

Ask your child where else in her body she might notice her breath (she might suggest her neck and shoulders, or somewhere she can feel her pulse). Together, experiment with the different places in your bodies where you can really notice the sensations of breathing in and breathing out.

After trying to find all the different places in the body where the breath can be felt, talk about which one was easiest to notice. This place in the body can be an anchor for your child's attention—when she is feeling distracted or unfocused, she can narrow her attention to one aspect of the breath.

IN THE MOMENT

Remind your child of her anchor. First model deep breathing while placing your hand on your chest (or wherever your child's anchor spot is). After a moment, say, "Can you notice your breath in your chest?" This question can interrupt the chaos that your child has been pulled into. It's also an invitation to your child to notice a part of her experience, rather than a command to "Breathe!", which may be met with more resistance.

VARIATIONS FOR AGES 3-6

• If the concept of an anchor is a bit difficult for your child to grasp, try playing a game in which you try to breathe like different types of animals (a lion with deep roaring breaths, a bunny with short sniffing breaths, or a dragon with big, fiery exhales, for example) and then talk about what it feels like inside their body when they do it.

• It's often easier for younger kids to notice the movement of their body in relationship to the breath if they are lying down. Ask your child to lie down and place her hands on her chest and then her stomach as she breathes (see the Belly Breathing exercise on page 32).

VARIATION FOR AGES 7-11

• Invite your older child to experiment with different ways of noticing her breath. She may find it helpful to count her breaths (up to the number 10, and then starting over again), or saying the words "in" and "out" in her head as she breathes. Encourage her to find the "style" of mindful breathing that feels most natural.

More to Explore

• What did it feel like to spend a few moments just noticing your breath? (Children often report that it felt calming or relaxing—you can point out to them how easy it can be to just focus on a specific part of their breath during the day when they need to relax.) When during the day do you think it would help you to pause and take a few deep breaths? (Many children find it helpful before bed.)

• Many smartwatches and phone apps have timed breathing exercises—try downloading an app like Stop, Breathe, and Think or Smiling Mind and setting aside a few minutes each day for mindful breathing.

• Mindful breathing is a core mindfulness practice and one that you can continue working on with your child. Start with just 30 seconds at a time, and gradually increase how much time you spend sitting in silence and noticing the breath. Make it a fun game to see how much time you can get up to on the timer!

MINDFUL LISTENING

Children may have a hard time listening carefully, as there are often so many other compelling distractions. This exercise will help your child develop listening skills. Every time we practice listening to something, and filtering out the distracting stimuli, we strengthen the neural connections in our brains that are responsible for paying attention.

TRY THIS TOGETHER

The instruction is simple: you are going to ring the bell, and then your child will try to listen carefully to the entire sound of the bell. Ask her if she can notice the exact moment when she can no longer hear any resonating sound from the bell.

You can try a few variations: asking her to listen with eyes open then closed, asking her to ring the bell for you, or, after a few times of listening to the bell, simply listening to what things sound like when you don't ring the bell.

YOU WILL NEED

A bell or a chime, or even an app that can make a resonant bell sound. Ideally use something that makes a ringing noise, so that the sound continues to reverberate and linger.

IN THE MOMENT

Mindful listening is a great way to interrupt a negative thought spiral or an impending meltdown. Listening quite literally gets our children "out of their heads" and brings them to the present moment by focusing on external stimuli. As children learn to FOCUS, they discover that they can choose where to direct their attention. If your child is starting to feel overwhelmed by thoughts or emotions, ask her to notice three things she can hear right now. And then notice if and how that shifts the situation.

VARIATIONS FOR AGES 3-6

• Make mindful listening into a game where you gather some of your child's toys (that make noise) and ask her to close her eyes and guess which toy it is.

• Fill plastic containers or small boxes with various items to make shakers (rice, buttons, beads, dry beans, salt, small rocks, etc.). Make two of each kind. As you shake one of the shakers, your child can listen carefully to the sound and find the other one that matches yours.

• Close your eyes and, without ringing the bell, see if you can identify five things that you hear.

VARIATIONS FOR AGES 7-11

• Ask your older child what it's like to listen at school. Does she notice that her attention wanders sometimes? If it does, reassure her that it's totally normal. Talk about how she could use her mindful listening at school, really focusing on the words the teacher is saying and staying with them.

• Play some music and ask your child to really listen to it: what instruments can she hear? Can she understand all the lyrics? How does the music make her feel? Do different thoughts pop into her head while she's listening?

• While mindful listening is primarily an exercise in paying attention, we may also notice how quickly our judgmental mind gets involved in the game. You can discuss with your child if she noticed judgments like "This is a pleasant sound" or "Why is it so noisy outside? I just want it to be quiet so I can listen to the bell!" Explain to her that mindfulness is a way of seeing how our mind works and how much time we often spend getting wrapped up in how much we like or dislike something.

More to Explore

• Was mindful listening easy or hard? What other sounds could you hear? When else could you try practicing mindful listening (at home, at school, when you're having a conversation)? How did it feel to listen mindfully?

• Your child may report that she felt calm, relaxed, tired, bored, or something else while doing this. Any reaction or response is fine. Mindfulness is simply about noticing what is happening in this moment.

MINDFUL SEEING

The purpose of this exercise is to encourage your child to really see. Sometimes we see not what is actually in front of us, but what our mind tells us is in front of us! This activity is all about getting really detailed about the information that we are taking in with our eyes.

TRY THIS TOGETHER

Tell your child that she is going to imagine that she is a friendly alien who has never seen an earthling child's bedroom before. She has just landed in the bedroom and is trying to figure out what she is seeing.

Invite your child to see her bedroom as this friendly alien might, with lots of curiosity and attention. Because this alien has never been to Earth before, he doesn't know the words for anything, so he can't say, "Oh, that's a bed." He might say something like, "Hmm… this big, fluffy thing has lots of colors—red, blue, and orange—and it's really soft." Or he might look at a clock and describe it as "something round and shiny with scribbles on it."

See if your child can describe ten items in her room with this attention to detail. How many pencil crayons are in her pot? How many different colors are there? Can she describe her teddy bear in detail? What words would she use?

More to Explore

• Ask your child to use her mindful eyes to see if she can notice five things she has never actually noticed before in her room (for example, she may notice a unique marking in the wood floor or a small detail in a piece of art on the wall). If she does identify things, talk about how we can get so used to being in a place that we stop paying attention to it! What is it like when we put our mindful eyes on?

• You could try this activity anywhere that is a familiar place, such as at school or at a friend's house, and when she is outside in the garden or park, can she use her mindful eyes to really connect with nature?

• What would it be like if we paid attention with our eyes like this all the time?

IN THE MOMENT

Any practice that draws attention away from whatever is causing a freak out can be helpful in a difficult moment. In this practice, your child can shift attention from something unpleasant to a more neutral anchor. When your child is overwhelmed, try giving her a mindful seeing challenge. For example, ask her to pause and find three things in the room that are blue, or four things that are square. This momentary distraction can interrupt the feelings of distress and allow your child to regain a bit of control. This shifting of attention from her internal chaos to her external environment can be very soothing. Once she's placed her attention elsewhere, your child may realize that the original stressor wasn't all that bad, or she may have calmed down just enough to process the event more calmly.

OH, THOSE DISTRACTIONS!

An important skill to cultivate is the ability to stay focused on something when there are lots of distractions. In this activity, you and your child will make a game out of trying to distract each other!

TRY THIS TOGETHER

Give your child an age-appropriate, fun, or slightly challenging task to focus on. For a younger child, this might be coloring, building a block tower, or sorting objects by shape or color. For an older child, it might be trying to count backward in her head, read a short book, or count her breaths.

Give your child a moment to settle in to her activity, with the gentle instruction to try to focus on what she is doing (but letting her know that you might try to distract her!). After a minute or so, create some not-too-noisy distractions—tapping your nails, humming a song, talking—and notice how your child responds. Continue off and on for about a minute, and then switch roles—this time you do something and your child distracts you.

After you've each had a turn, talk about what that was like. How difficult was it to maintain focus? If it was hard, what made it hard? (You might talk about how our innate curiosity makes us want to find the source of the sound or know what the conversation might be about, or how our mind can very quickly start creating a story about what is happening.)

Was it frustrating to have these distractions in the background? Notice if you tensed up, got angry, or had some kind of physical reaction to being distracted. What did you do when that happened?

What would it be like to just let the distractions be there in the background? Could you try to notice your curiosity or your frustration, and still continue to work on your original task?

Begin the activity again, trying to maintain focus through distractions as each of you take a turn. When you're done, talk about what, if anything, was different the second time.

YOU WILL NEED

A simple activity for you and your child to do (see examples below)

VARIATION FOR AGES 3-6

• If your younger child finds being distracted by you too frustrating, try doing a simple activity like coloring together. First, do it with something slightly distracting in the background, like having the TV on or a song playing on the radio. Then turn off the distraction and continue with the activity. Talk to your child about what it's like to do something with distractions, and without distractions.

VARIATIONS FOR AGES 7-11

• If your child found this exercise difficult, ask her if concentrating was difficult because the noise or activity itself created too much interference, or if it was more her reaction to the distractions (getting frustrated, being curious about what was happening elsewhere). Would it be possible to do that activity even with the distractions?

• Talk about how a distraction (or any minor irritation) can be frustrating on two levels: the actual disruption, and then our irritation at being interrupted. Invite your child to try to notice in the next few days how she responds to interruptions.

More to Explore

• It's interesting to have a conversation with your child about how often she gets distracted during the day. What kinds of things usually bother her? What are the distractions that she can't control, and needs to find a way to work with? Which distractions CAN she control and how could she eliminate them?

• If your child does identify things that continually interfere with her concentration that she can control, ask her to eliminate that distraction for a week and then see what she notices. (This can be great for kids that struggle with being distracted while they are doing their homework.)

ATTENTION: microscope and telescope

A crucial way of paying attention is being able to move from a narrow focus to a broad focus. For example, your child may need to shift her attention from doing her classwork to focusing on the teacher. By practicing "microscoping" and "telescoping" her attention, she'll learn to focus on details while maintaining awareness of her surroundings.

TRY THIS TOGETHER

Assuming you've done some of the other exercises in this chapter, talk to your child about how she has already learned lots of different ways of paying attention and various things she can notice—her breath, sounds, body, things she can see. Remind her that paying attention is something that she is doing all day long! Ask her what kind of things she needs to be aware of and notice throughout the day. Depending on your child's age, help her to generate a list of things that require a very narrow focus, like reading books, playing with small toys, brushing her teeth, doing homework, or washing dirt or markers off her hands, and things that require a broader attention, like having a conversation with several people, or walking outside and being aware of traffic and surroundings.

Tell her that you're going to practice paying attention to little things and big things today, so we're going to pretend we have a microscope and a telescope to help us.

You can read the following to your child while she sits or lies down:

Take a few breaths and just notice what your breath feels like in your anchor spot (see page 48)…

On your next breath, turn your attention to your body, noticing how it feels right now…

On the next breath, see if you can bring your attention to your legs… and now just your left leg… and now just your left knee…

YOU WILL NEED

It can help to find pictures (from a science book or online) of microscopes and telescopes so your child understands what they are and how they work

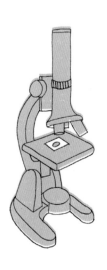

Now see if you can notice just the back of your left knee… Imagine you have your microscope with you, and that it allows your attention to notice the smallest little sensations or feelings just in this small spot on your body… See if you can focus your attention even further, noticing just a tiny little part of the back of your knee… What does it feel like to have such a narrow window of attention?

On your next breath, slowly bring your attention back to your whole knee… to your whole left leg, to your whole body… and back to your breath in your anchor spot. Imagine setting aside your microscope so you can let your attention get even bigger…

On your next breath, see if you can pay attention to everything around you… even with your eyes closed… Can you feel what you are sitting or lying on? Can you feel the temperature of the air in the room? Can you hear any sounds in the room?

Now imagine that your telescope is letting your attention get even bigger… Can you notice anything outside of the room? Any sounds? Let your mind imagine what is outside this room right now and outside the house right now… what the weather is like… what might be happening outside…

On your next breath, let your telescope go even further… imagine your attention being as big as the sky… you can see clouds and birds and the tops of the trees… What does it feel like now to have such a big window of attention?

On your next breath, you can start bringing your attention back in, like you're adjusting the telescope lens… bringing your attention back to what's outside the house right now… back to this room… and back to your body and your breath.

Take a few more deep breaths and open your eyes.

VARIATIONS FOR AGES 3-6

• For younger children, you'll want to do a shorter, more concrete version of this exercise. Ask them to notice a very small, specific place in their body (their big toe, for example), and then notice their entire body.

• If noticing sensations in their body is too difficult or abstract, you could do a variation of this outside. Lie down on the ground and look up at the sky, noticing how big it is and how there is so much to see at once. Then look at a small blade of grass or an insect, noticing how close we have to get to it to really see it. Which does your child enjoy more, looking at the big sky or the small things around her? Talk about how we have to pay attention to different things in different ways!

VARIATION FOR AGES 7-11

• Talk to your child about how this practice might help her at school, when she has to shift her attention throughout the day.

More to Explore

For some children, practicing mindfulness with a wide, open attention feels more calming; for others, it feels better to focus on something quite small. Talk to your child about which way of paying attention felt better.

CHAPTER 4

FEEL *Developing Emotional Awareness and Self-Regulation*

Emotional awareness and self-regulation are crucial skills for children. In order to function and be emotionally healthy, we need to be able to identify what we are feeling when we are feeling it, and determine what would be an appropriate action to take in response to our emotion. With mindfulness, your child can become more adept at recognizing his emotions as they arise. Once he can name and understand his feelings, he can learn self-regulation. This means he can experience strong emotions without being overwhelmed by them, he can calm himself down when he's upset, and he can carefully respond to situations instead of merely reacting to them out of frustration.

As you approach the activities in this chapter, it's helpful to remember that our children often feel their emotions quite intensely. They don't have the years of wisdom or experience that remind them that "this isn't a big deal" or that "this, too, shall pass." For children, their present moment experience IS a big deal. They are working with big feelings in their little bodies. It's our role as parents to guide them through their complicated emotional terrain.

A fun way to introduce emotional awareness to your child is to ask them to imagine what it would be like if they didn't have emotions. Though sometimes we may wish we didn't have to experience sadness or frustration, we can appreciate that emotions

are what give meaning and texture to our lives. Our feelings are an important part of our human experience… so we might as well learn how to work with them, not against them!

In this chapter, you'll learn practices that will help your child become familiar with his internal emotional landscape, develop an emotional vocabulary, and cultivate the ability to tolerate difficult and unpleasant emotions.

Important note: When talking about emotions with your child, be careful to avoid labeling certain emotions as "good," and others as "bad" (or even "positive" or "negative"). From a mindfulness perspective, no emotion is inherently good or bad. All emotions are information, letting us know that something in our environment needs our attention. If an emotion feels unpleasant, it will prompt us to take action to feel better, and if feels pleasant, it may prompt us to savor the experience. Remind your child that all emotions are allowed… because they are already here! The important thing is that we notice them, and respond to them in ways that are safe for ourselves and for others.

EMOTION CHARADES

This is a fun game to help kids understand how their feelings show up in their bodies.

YOU WILL NEED

Pieces of paper or index cards with the following emotions written down on them (one emotion per sheet/card): happy, sad, angry, excited, scared, worried, peaceful (or any other emotions you'd like to add)

TRY THIS TOGETHER

Play the game like regular charades: when someone draws a card, they have to act out the emotion without making any sounds. Encourage your child to show the emotion on his face AND in his body.

Usually, it doesn't take very long for people to guess an emotion. You could talk with your child about why that is—ie. it's really important for us, as social creatures, to be able to read emotions and communicate our emotions to others. We've already had lots of practice with doing this throughout our life!

First and foremost, have fun playing this game with your child, but then take the time to talk about each emotion. What happens to your body when you feel this way? For example, children often notice that their bodies get tight and small when they are angry, their bodies feel heavy and contracted when they are sad, and they feel lighter and relaxed and expansive when they are happy. Rather than focusing on whether the emotion feels "good" or "bad," ask your child if it feels pleasant or unpleasant. Do some of the emotions look and feel the same (for example, scared and worried)? How is each emotion a little bit different in how it shows up in your body? Why do you think that emotion makes us feel that way?

IN THE MOMENT

You're not going to start playing charades when your child is having a meltdown, but if you notice him starting to get upset, you could say something like, "Oh, it kind of looks like your body is angry. Can you feel that?" This can be a powerful way of coaching your child to recognize an emotion before it becomes too much for him to handle.

VARIATIONS FOR AGES 3-6

• Print out images of emojis for the emotion cards for children who are too young to read.

• It may be easier to demonstrate a few basic emotions to a younger child, such as happy, sad, afraid, angry, or do them alongside them at the same time. You could model how these emotions show up for you (for example, a frown on your face and your head down for "sad") or how your child often looks and behaves when he is experiencing these emotions (for example, clenching your fists and stomping your feet for "angry").

VARIATIONS FOR AGES 7-11

• Instead of using emotion cards, ask your child to demonstrate an emotion that he felt today, then talk about what happened!

• Talk to your child about each emotion, and how there isn't really such a thing as a "negative emotion." All feelings are important and valid— they are information! When we have these strong sensations in our body, it's a way of telling us that something needs our attention. It's our body saying, "Something important is happening! Pay attention!" Talk about how emotions often create an urge to take a particular action (run, hit, smile, cry, yell, etc.). Why does your child think that is?

More to Explore

Talk with your child about how our emotions show up not just on our face (like an emoji), but in our entire body. What were the physical clues in his body about what the emotion was? What did he notice in his hands, or arms, or legs, or anywhere else? Did these physical sensations help him better understand what he was feeling? (This conversation is a good segue into the next activity.)

MY AMAZING EMOTIONS

It can be hard for kids to identify what they're feeling (it's hard for adults, too!), so this activity helps them to explore an emotion by understanding how it shows up in their body and their mind.

TRY THIS TOGETHER

Ask your child to think about a time recently when he had a really strong emotion. This may be easy for him to remember, or you may want to cue him with a recent example of when he was upset, or happy, or disappointed, or something else. Try to pick an event that was memorable, but not too intense; something around a 3 or 4 on a scale of 1–10.

Ask your child to close his eyes and remember the event that led to this emotion. What had he been doing that day? How did he feel earlier in the day (if he can remember)?

As he thinks about the event that led to this feeling (you may need to describe the episode to a younger child), what was his immediate reaction? Did the event feel positive or negative, good or bad?

What did he notice in his body? Even in remembering an emotion, the feeling can show up physically. What expression did he have on his face? What are his arms, hands, legs, and feet doing? What does he feel in his belly? Where does this feeling seem to "be" in his body?

Where does this feeling NOT show up in his body? Where in his body feels okay? On a subtle level, this question helps your child understand that his body is big enough to hold a difficult emotion; even though it shows up physically, it doesn't take over his entire body.

What thoughts does he notice? As your child spends some time observing this emotion, does it change at all? Does it get less intense, or more intense, or does it stay the same? (Many children will notice that it changes; this is a helpful way to point out that emotions are not "solid," but that they ebb and flow and shift over time, even over just a few seconds!)

Finally, you could ask your child to remember what he did when he was feeling this way. **Did he do something that helped him feel better?** Did he do something that he wished that he hadn't done? (Again, all answers are fine; this is a helpful way to learn from experience!)

What might your child do the next time he feels this way?

VARIATIONS FOR AGES 3-6

• Some of the questions might be difficult for younger children to process. Here are some alternative questions to help them understand their emotions, such as:

—If this emotion were an animal, what kind of animal would it be? What would its name be? What would it do? What would help it to calm down?

—If this emotion were a color, what would it be?

—If this emotion had a smell, what would it be?

—If this emotion could make a sound, what sound would it make?

• Take pictures of your child demonstrating his various emotions—sad, happy, angry, excited, afraid, worried. Print out the pictures and use them to make an Emotion Dictionary. Create a page for each emotion. You could search online for images of stick figures and include them on each page, having your child identify where he notices that feeling in his body.

IN THE MOMENT

If you asked your child to identify and compare his emotion to something (see above), you can reference it when you see it arise. For example, you might say, "Oh, is Joe the angry gorilla here?" **This way of seeing the emotion as a separate entity allows your child to distance himself from the feeling,** realizing that it is not "him." If you also had previously asked your child what might calm "Joe the Gorilla" down, you could ask your child to help "soothe Joe" when you see he is angry.

I once worked with a child who identified his frustration as a koala named Sam; the koala could be calmed down by being given a leaf to eat. So when this child felt frustrated, he would close his eyes and imagine he was feeding a leaf to Sam the koala, and it would help him soothe his frustration!

READING EMOTIONS

Sometimes our children have difficulty talking about their feelings because they aren't able to put them into words. In this activity, you'll explore the emotions of others as a way of developing your child's emotional vocabulary.

YOU WILL NEED

Age-appropriate children's books

TRY THIS TOGETHER

Read a book to your child, and take some time to pause during parts of the story to ask him what emotion he thinks a character is experiencing. Ask your child why he thinks the character is feeling that way (what clues did he pick up on in the character's face, body language, spoken language, or the events that had happened to them?). Ask your child if he has ever felt that same emotion, and what it felt like. What other words could he use to describe the feeling? (You could also use similar questions to the ones in the previous activity.) If appropriate, talk to your child about what that emotion is like for you.

How does the character in the story respond to his emotion? Does he make a choice that is skillful? Why does your child think he acted the way he did? How were other people affected by the actions of the main character? If someone in the story acts out in anger, ask your child how he would feel if he was treated that way.

IN THE MOMENT

If your child's current distress is similar to something that happened in a story you have read together, you could remind your child of the character in the book. For example, you might say "Are you feeling like Robbie felt when he lost his toy?" This can help your child distance himself a little from his immediate sense of overwhelm.

You can also ask similar questions of your child if you see another child at the playground who is upset, or if you are watching a movie together. See if you both agree about what may have angered the character or person, and if you both identify with the same emotion.

See if you can find natural ways to introduce emotional words and concepts to your child. Every time you have a conversation with him about feelings, you are developing his emotional vocabulary and understanding.

More to Explore

A great movie to watch together and discuss emotions is *Inside Out*. In this popular children's film from Pixar, the five basic emotions of Joy, Sadness, Anger, Disgust, and Fear are depicted as characters inside a young girl's mind. The movie helps children see how each emotion plays an important role in helping them be safe, happy, and connected. After watching the movie, you could talk to your child about how those emotions show up for them throughout the day. Ask him to think about the other emotions he notices inside his brain besides the five shown in the movie.

A TEXT FROM MY BRAIN

In this activity, you will use emojis as a fun and simple way to talk about emotions with your child.

YOU WILL NEED

• Emojis on your phone or printed pictures of them

• Paper and crayons/markers

TRY THIS TOGETHER

There are many ways to use emojis to explore emotions. Try doing any or all of the activities below with your child:

• Look at pictures of common emojis, and ask your child to identify the emotion in each one. As with the emotion charades game (see page 62), ask your child how he knows that is the feeling the emoji represents. What are the clues? You could also ask your child to speculate why someone might feel that way. What might have happened to him or her? Ask him, "What makes you feel that way?"

• Ask your child to tell the story of his day in emojis. Ask him to create a text message, or draw pictures of various emojis that would summarize the day's events.

• Ask him, "If your brain could text you right now, what would the text say? What emojis would be in the message?"

• Ask him, "Which emoji showed up the most for you today?"

• Ask him to draw his own emoji to show how he is feeling right now.

IN THE MOMENT

If your child is having a difficult moment, and you can catch it early, stop and ask him what his brain would text him right now? What's your emoji right now? This can be a silly way to interrupt a tantrum and allow your child to name his feeling.

HOLDING MY EMOTIONS

This activity introduces your child to containment, in which we create the space to hold our emotion in our awareness. We contain it not by suppressing it, but by watching it unfold without letting it overwhelm us.

TRY THIS TOGETHER

Introduce this activity by talking to your child about how our emotions can sometimes feel really big and overpowering. (It might help to gently remind your child about a recent experience he had with a powerful emotion). When our emotions feel this way, sometimes it's like they just explode right out of us and we feel like we can't control them. But wouldn't it be nice if we could learn how to experience our emotions without feeling overwhelmed? Wouldn't it be helpful if we could be patient with our feelings?

Explain that when we are mindful, we are able to pay attention to our emotions, and watch them just like we watch our breath or our thoughts. (Remind your child about how you watched your thoughts settle in the mind jar.) Can we try that with our emotions?

Our emotions often feel a lot "stickier" than our thoughts, but you can share with your child that emotions usually only last about 90 seconds! Our surge of anger, or frustration, or sadness takes less than two minutes to work its way through our body, creating various sensations and experiences. That's not a very

YOU WILL NEED

Use your mind jar if you made one (see page 46)

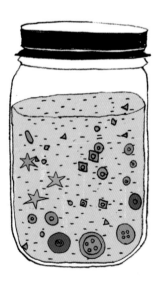

long time… so if we can be patient with our feeling, and watch it swirl around in us the way the glitter swirls around in our mind jar, we can contain it.

What would happen if we didn't have a lid on our mind jar and we shook it up? It would explode! And that can happen when we don't pay attention to our feelings— they can leak out everywhere and things get really messy! When we pay attention to our feelings, we don't push them away or pretend they're not there, we just watch them. We remind ourselves that the emotion won't last very long, and we watch it swirl around our body and mind… and then we watch it settle.

Ask your child what emotion he often has a hard time holding or watching, and ask him to think of a time when he felt that way. For example, ask your child to think of a time when he experienced a particular emotion, such as stress, anger, sadness, and read the scripts on the opposite page.

IN THE MOMENT

When your child is in the grip of a strong emotion, remind him about being patient with his emotion. One way he can hold his emotion in awareness is by breaking it down into its component parts; the very fact that he is overwhelmed is probably a sign that he's experiencing all aspects of the emotion at once.

To help your child contain his emotion, ask him to take a deep breath and guide him to…

• Notice the sensations that are present in his body right now…

• Notice the thoughts in his head right now…

• Notice the feelings he is having right now…

• Notice if this moment feels pleasant or unpleasant…

(Repeat the instructions if necessary.)

In this practice, your child can notice tightness, clenching, a fast pulse, a thought, a feeling of frustration, a pounding in his head, an unpleasant sensation, a thought about yelling… and he may begin to slowly settle down as he contains the emotion by recognizing its component parts, instead of drowning in the overwhelming experience of "anger."

Stressed

• Imagine that the glitter in the jar is all of the stressful feelings rushing around your body… It's okay if you're feeling stressed. We all feel stressed sometimes. Stress is your body's way of letting you know something needs your attention right now.

• Notice your hands. Are they clenched?

• Notice your stomach. How does it feel?

• Notice your face. Is it relaxed, or are you clenching your teeth? Are your eyes relaxed?

• Notice your thoughts. Do you notice worries? Can you just let the worries be there? They're just worries… they're not actually true.

• Notice what it feels like to be patient with your stress. Does it feel any different now that you've given the stress a bit of time to settle?

Angry

• Imagine that the glitter in the jar is all of the angry feelings rushing around your body… It's okay if you're feeling angry. We all do at times. Anger is your body's way of letting you know something needs your attention right now.

• Notice your hands. Are they clenched or tight? Are they moving or still?

• Notice your shoulders. Are they relaxed or are they hunched?

• Notice your face. Is it relaxed, or are you clenching your teeth? Are your eyes relaxed?

• Notice your thoughts. Does it sound like your thoughts are yelling? Are they loud or soft?

• Notice what it feels like to be patient with your anger. Does it feel any different now that you've given the anger time to settle?

Sad

• Imagine that the glitter in the jar is all of the sad feelings in your body… It's okay if you're feeling sad. We all feel sad sometimes. Sadness is your body's way of letting you know something needs your attention right now. It's letting you know you need to take care of yourself right now.

• Notice your body. Does it feel heavy? Can you bring your attention to your heart? What does it feel like in your chest right now?

• Notice your face. Does your face feel heavy?

• Notice your thoughts. What are you thinking about right now? Are you thinking about memories? Are you thinking about how much you miss someone? Are you thinking about your friends?

• Notice what it feels like to be patient with your sadness. Does it feel any different now that you've given the sadness time to settle?

Ask your child to imagine that the glitter in the jar is all the feelings rushing around his body as he shakes the jar… and then take some deep breaths with him and watch the glitter settle. Even though our emotions can feel more powerful than our thoughts, they will settle down, too, if we give them the chance.

CHAPTER 5

PAUSE *Making Wise Choices*

Psychologist Victor Frankl believed that between every stimulus and reaction there could be a space, a *pause*. And during that pause, we could consider many possible *responses*, instead of reacting based on habit. Frankl believed it was in that space, the moment of observation and choice, that we could experience profound growth.

This chapter is about the space, the incredibly important pause between stimulus and response. In the previous chapter, your child learned the first step in self-regulation: the ability to notice her feelings and notice if she has been triggered by an unpleasant stimulus.

But just because she's noticed her anger or frustration in this moment doesn't mean she knows what to do in the next moment to make a wise choice. Before beginning the exercises in this chapter, it may be helpful to refer back to the strategies your child learned for soothing herself in Chapter 2. Once your child has her toolbox of calming practices, she can utilize the cognitive strategies in this chapter to work skillfully with her emotions. These exercises involve the development of metacognition: the ability to think about one's thinking.

Some researchers estimate that we have somewhere between 50,000–70,000 thoughts in a day. Our thoughts have a profound impact on our emotions and our perceptions. And while thinking is incredibly useful, you can probably also think of a time in your life when all the thinking you were engaged in didn't really help you– and, in fact, likely made a situation worse. It was probably a time when you told yourself a one-sided story, made assumptions that weren't true, or based a decision on interpretations that were not accurate. This capacity for observing thoughts and objectively reflecting on them is one that children continue to develop throughout adolescence and into early adulthood. The activities in this chapter are fun ways to introduce these concepts to your child and lay the foundation for her further cognitive development.

In this chapter, you will learn simple practices for teaching your child how her brain works. You'll also learn ways you can help your child investigate her thoughts, and understand when she is lost in a story that may not actually be true about the situation she is experiencing. She'll learn how to see things from others' perspectives, and how she can choose acceptable behavior in difficult situations.

NEURAL WI-FI

This is a fun activity that introduces kids to what happens in their brain when they get upset. They can learn how to restore the connectivity of their "neural Wi-Fi" to ensure that the rational, wise part of their brain can easily communicate with the emotional and reactive center of the brain.

TRY THIS TOGETHER

Begin by asking your child if she has ever been so angry or upset that she has said or done something that she later regretted. Most children can relate to this universal experience. If you'd like, share a story about a time when this happened to you, or invite your child to tell you her experience. Explain that you want to talk to her about why we sometimes act in ways that we know we shouldn't. You're going to explain a few important things about her brain, so that she can understand what's happening inside her head during these times.

Make a fist with your hand, with your thumb folded on the inside. Explain to your child that from the side, your fist kind of makes the shape of the human brain. The space between your first and second knuckles is the forehead, your fingernails are about where the eyes are, and your wrist is the back of the skull where your head connects to the rest of the body. Have your child make a fist in this way, too.

Now you can teach your child about two important parts of her brain. The first part is right behind her forehead, and it's called the pre-frontal cortex (the PFC). We use this part of the brain to consider the consequences of our actions and so it helps us make good choices. You could liken it to a wise teacher, reminding you of how others want to be treated, or helping you see that whatever is upsetting you maybe isn't that big of a deal.

Now open up your hand to reveal your thumb. Explain that your thumb represents an inner part of the brain called the

amygdala. This is the emotional—or "freak out"—center of the brain! When you are upset, scared, angry, worried, or excited, this part of the brain is active.

Ask your child if she thinks it's a good idea to have a freak-out center in her brain. While freaking out may not feel very good, it's actually quite important to have a place inside our brain that warns us if something is wrong or if we need to take immediate action. The amygdala is like the guard dog that lets us know if we are unsafe. It's very helpful… but sometimes it can be hard if the dog gets upset over little things that actually aren't a big deal!

Fold your hand back into a fist and point out how normally the wise teacher and the guard dog are really close together in your brain. They can send messages to each other! It's like you have Wi-Fi in your brain that allows all the parts to communicate. If the connectivity is good, when the guard dog freaks out, he sends a message to the teacher that something is wrong, and the teacher can quickly assess what's happening and help you make a wise choice.

But what happens if the Wi-Fi goes down and they can't talk?

The guard dog is barking and growling so loud that the teacher can't concentrate or think! Even if the teacher tried to tell the dog that everything was okay, he wouldn't be able to hear him. (Dan Siegel calls this "flipping your lid"— see resources on page 124 for more details. You can demonstrate this by flipping open your fist to show that the amygdala and pre-frontal cortex are no longer touching and communicating—the connection is broken). Ask your child if she sometimes feels so scared or angry that she can't think straight. Does it

IN THE MOMENT

Once you've introduced these concepts to your child, you can ask her guiding questions when she starts to get upset: Is your guard dog starting to freak out? What will help him calm down? What is the wise teacher trying to say?

If your child is so upset that no words are going to help, you could simply demonstrate the hand model of your brain as a signal that your child needs to get the neural Wi-Fi back up and running. Perhaps show a brain with a "flipped lid," and take a few deep breaths yourself, slowly putting the lid back on as you do so.

sometimes feel like her emotions are too overwhelming to handle? This is what's happening in your brain when you feel that way! The challenge is to get the Wi-Fi back up and running so you can get back in control.

If your child has identified exercises from the previous chapters that help her to feel calm and relaxed, you could do those together now—perhaps Belly Breathing (see page 32), My Safe Place (see page 42), or the Tension Tamer (see page 34). As you do the exercise, slowly bring one finger down at a time, re-forming the fist/brain with everything connected and communicating. (You can call this "un-flipping your lid.")

Now you have a strategy to reconnect your brain's "Wi-Fi," when you recognize frustration or anger you can pause and let your PFC (or wise teacher) get back in control.

VARIATION FOR AGES 3-6

• This activity is best suited for children ages 6 and up, but you can talk to younger children about how they feel when they get angry or upset, and whether feeling this way makes it easier or harder to think. Depending on your child's level of understanding, you could explain that there are different parts of her brain that handle her feelings, and help her to make choices. If she can first focus on soothing her upset feeling, then she can try to make a good choice. Explain that it's hard to do both at the same time!

VARIATIONS FOR AGES 7-11

• Most kids love learning about their brain. Find a simple outline image of the brain online and label the location of the PFC and the amygdala. Encourage your child to envision these parts of her brain communicating with her "neural Wi-Fi" when she gets upset.

• You can explore the "neural Wi-Fi" analogy even further with older children. Show them a picture of the neural networks in their brain, and how they actually communicate via electrical messages.

More to Explore

When you "flip your lid," or when your guard dog starts panicking, what are the things that you can do to calm down and get the neural Wi-Fi back up and running?

THE TV SHOW IN MY HEAD

With mindfulness children can see their thoughts clearly and determine which are helpful, and which are not. There are many different analogies for thoughts coming and going, such as clouds passing through the sky, or boats sailing down a river. Here we imagine thoughts like a TV show in our mind. With mindfulness, we can distance ourselves from our thoughts by seeing them as separate from us.

TRY THIS TOGETHER

Ask your child to imagine that she is watching her favorite TV show, and it's an episode that she really likes. Does she ever get so "into" the show that she almost feels like she is part of it— that she is experiencing the events and sharing the feelings with the characters? That the TV show feels totally "real"? And then something happens—maybe she hears a sound or someone calls her name—and she remembers that she's just sitting here on the couch and the TV show is just playing out on the TV? (Most kids—and adults—can relate to this experience, although you may need to adjust this explanation if your child is younger.)

Explain that our thoughts are kind of like a TV show in our head... playing one episode after another. Sometimes we get so "into" our thoughts that we get wrapped up in them in the same

If your child seems to be stuck in a difficult thought,
or says something self-critical, ask her, "Do you have your thought
remote? Do you need to press mute, pause, play, or record?"

way we get caught up in a TV show. Our thoughts seem so powerful and real and we just assume that everything we are thinking is true. We might think we need to follow every thought that comes up.

But what if we could step back from our thoughts a bit and imagine that they are like a TV show? Even though they are really intense and convincing, we don't have to believe them, just the way we don't have to believe that everything that is happening on a TV show is real.

When we stop and notice our thoughts, we have a choice about what we do with them. Just like with a TV show, you have a couple options on your remote for your brain:

MUTE: While it's pretty hard (in fact, impossible!) to stop thinking, you can decide that you don't need to pay attention to a thought. When you press the MUTE button on your thought, you allow yourself to turn your attention to something else. For example, if you are feeling frustrated and notice the thought, "I'm so bad at science! I'll never understand this!" you can "mute" the thought by turning your attention back to your assignment, and maybe tell yourself that you could ask your teacher for help. Just because the thought is there doesn't mean you have to listen to it.

PAUSE: Sometimes you might realize that a thought is important, but you need a minute to calm down before you are ready to think about it. In the same way you can pause a TV show and finish watching it later, you can pause your thought. Press pause, take a deep breath, notice what you can feel in your body, or use your favorite relaxation practice. Then, when you're ready, you can press…

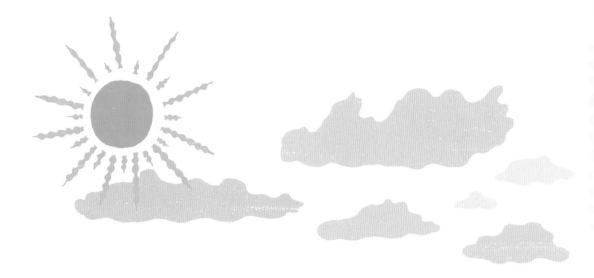

PLAY: Now you can watch your thought, imagining that you are sitting on the couch and watching this thought play out in your head. Pay attention to the words in your head and any pictures or images that are in your mind as you watch this thought. Notice how the thought makes you feel. Imagine watching the thought on a TV show in your mind. Based on what you are seeing, is your thought accurate? If your thought was "I'm so bad at science!," maybe after pausing and watching what's happening, you realize that no, you're not "bad," you're just struggling with this assignment.

DVR/RECORD: Sometimes we get so wrapped up in the TV show we never have that moment when we realize, "Aha! I was just totally sucked into this show that wasn't real!" Sometimes that happens with our thoughts, too. We got so wrapped up in them we weren't able to recognize that they were just thoughts, and that we could mute or pause or just watch them. That's okay! No one is perfect, and we all get caught up in thinking like this. (Perhaps share an example with your child of when this has happened to you.)

If that has happened, tell your child to imagine that she has recorded the thought. She can then "replay" it and ask herself "Was this thought true? How was it affecting me? If I have this kind of thought again, would it be helpful to mute it, pause it, or watch it?"

VARIATION FOR AGES 3–6

• As young children are just beginning to develop an awareness of their own thinking, noticing thoughts as separate events can be somewhat tricky. A fun exercise with young children is to invite them to close their eyes and focus on their breath, and then to notice the first thought that comes into their head. As soon as they notice their thought, ask them to share it with you. You can then ask them, depending on the thought, how it makes them feel, or if their thought is true. You can take turns doing this, just sharing with each other whatever thoughts pop into your mind. It's a great way to introduce young children to the constantly shifting contents of the mind.

VARIATIONS FOR AGES 7–11

• Reinforce to your child that mindfulness doesn't mean that we stop thinking, and we're certainly not saying that thinking is "bad." We're just recognizing that sometimes we get too caught up in thoughts, or sometimes our thoughts are not helpful, or are even self-critical.

• Ask your child, when does thinking help? When are thoughts not so helpful? What thoughts are the hardest to deal with? What would it be like to imagine your thoughts as simply a show in your mind, rather than things that are absolutely true and real?

More to Explore

Encourage your child to keep a "thought diary" for a week. (Younger kids can draw their thoughts instead of writing them down.) See if she notices that some of her thoughts are "re-runs," where the same thoughts keep playing on a loop. See if she notices which days of the week or which times of the day are more challenging for her based on the thoughts she is observing.

OH, THE STORIES WE TELL!

When we pay more attention to our thoughts, we notice how often we are wrapped up in stories: we take the incomplete information that is available to us at that moment, and create a tale that is part truth and part fiction about what is happening. In this activity, you'll help your child understand the way that she creates stories in her head and how those stories can be helpful, and sometimes can be harmful.

TRY THIS TOGETHER

Begin with about a minute (or more, if your child is willing) of mindful breathing. Offer the following guidance to your child:

Close your eyes, and bring your attention to your anchor (your body, your breath, or sounds)…

If you notice that your mind wanders away from your anchor, just allow it to wander… but watch where it goes…

If you notice thoughts, just watch them. What are the thoughts about?

Are the thoughts loud or soft?

Are the thoughts fast or slow?

Are the thoughts about you… about your friends… or about someone else?

For another moment, just notice any thoughts that pop into your head…

Take another deep breath, and open your eyes…

Ask your child to share the thoughts that she noticed. Often, the thoughts that pop into our head during what psychologists call "stimulus-independent thought," or "mind wandering," are about ourselves. When there's no pressing cognitive task at hand, we start telling "the story of me." Though your child's thoughts may have been about many different things, it's quite

YOU WILL NEED

Paper and markers/crayons/colored pencils/pens

likely that she was thinking about herself, her friends, what she was doing just now... and it's also quite likely that she was telling a story. If you notice any of these in what your child shares, point that out.

We have storytelling minds!

Your child probably loves to read or listen to stories. Explain to your child that as humans, we are storytelling creatures. People throughout history have gathered together to tell each other tales about the past or about their own lives. This is how we make sense of the world around us.

And though we may not be crafting novels in our head each day, we are telling stories. In any given moment, we're taking in what's around us and trying to fit it into a pattern or narrative.

Depending on the age of your child, ask her if she was telling a story just now in the thoughts she noticed. For younger children, you can emphasize that a story doesn't have to mean something elaborate; it could simply be, "Mommy is telling me to notice my breathing and I think it's kind of silly but mommy likes to do these games. I bet she's not thinking things right now... I'm thinking about the bunny we saw yesterday..."

As with our thinking in general, there is nothing wrong with our tendency to create stories. This is how the mind works, and it's how we make sense of the world. But sometimes, the stories we start to tell ourselves are not actually true. We might convince ourselves that someone else is acting a certain way just to be mean to us, when that might not be the case. We might think that the look on dad's face means he's mad, and then we create a story about why dad is mad at us... and then all of a sudden, this story we're telling is making us not feel very good!

Our thoughts, and our stories, are powerful!

Ask your child if she can think of a time when she started telling herself a story in her head, even though she didn't really have all the information to know if it was true. For example, she might have seen two classmates speaking to each

other and then glancing over at her, and then told herself that they were saying mean things about her. But then at recess, she found out that they were simply planning the game that they would play together. Perhaps you could share an example of a time when you have done this.

Researcher Brené Brown suggests a powerful strategy for when we're getting caught up in what she says could accurately be considered "conspiracy theories": stories

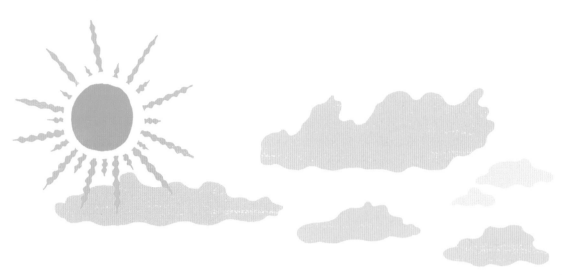

based on incomplete information. She says that when we notice our thoughts are churning, we should pause and say, "The story I'm telling myself right now is…" And then, as in the TV activity on page 77, we can ask if the story is actually true.

If your child gave you an example of a time when she was telling a story, ask if her version of the event was true. What would have happened if she had paused and observed the situation more clearly? What additional information would she need to be certain of her story? Would she have to adjust her story based on new information? Was there a part of the story that was a total guess? Again, you could share an example from when you had an incomplete story.

End by reminding your child that when she is overwhelmed and has remembered to PAUSE, a strategy she can use to make a good choice is to ask herself, "Am I telling myself a story right now? Is there more information I need? Is there a side to this that I am not seeing?"

IN THE MOMENT

Instead of asking your child, "What's the matter?" or "Why are you so upset?", try asking, "What story are you telling yourself right now?"

VARIATION FOR AGES 3-6

• There are great books that introduce young children to the idea that we often are only seeing a small part of what's happening, or that there are multiple ways to interpret something. My favorites are *Duck! Rabbit!* by Amy Krouse Rosenthal and Tom Lichtenheld, and *OH!* by Josse Goffin.

VARIATION FOR AGES 7-11

• After a family event (dinner, going to a movie or for a walk), ask everyone in the family to write a paragraph describing what happened. Then ask everyone to read aloud their descriptions. Notice the things that all the descriptions shared, but also the differences. Why do people often view the same events so differently?

More to Explore

Older children may enjoy learning more about the brain basis for this storytelling activity. Researchers have identified a part of the brain called the Default Mode Network (DMN). This is the part of the brain that is active when we don't have a task in front of us to focus on. One function of the DMN is to tell "the story of me." This means that when our minds wander, we tend to tell stories that help us make sense of our own lives. These stories are quite powerful because they help us see the structure and overall purpose in our life. Studies show that having a strong sense of the narrative story of our lives supports our wellbeing. Even though your child is quite young, it's a good idea to help her understand the important events in her life and what those events meant to her. Either through conversation or writing, encourage your child to reflect on the most significant events in her life. Why did she choose those events? What was meaningful about them? What did she learn from them?

Focusing on this aspect of the storytelling mind is a helpful way for older children to connect to their values. When they take their PAUSE moment, remembering what is important to them can help them connect to their values, and make a wiser choice.

I SAW

I SAW is a helpful acronym to guide your child through four simple steps when she is experiencing a difficult or overwhelming moment.

TRY THIS TOGETHER

Explain to your child that feelings of frustration or overwhelm or anger are entirely normal. It's okay to have whatever emotion she is noticing, but it is her responsibility to deal with that emotion in a way that is safe for herself and for others. When she notices a moment of frustration, she can use the I SAW technique. Explain each of the steps below.

I: I feel

The first step is to simply acknowledge what you are feeling! Take a deep breath and check in with the sensations in your body, and with your thoughts. Can you recognize the emotion you are experiencing? You can then silently say to yourself, "I feel angry," or "I feel sad."

S: Story

Are you telling yourself a story right now? How are you narrating or explaining what's happening? Just take a moment to review your story—no editing or telling yourself you shouldn't be feeling what you're feeling. Just notice the story.

A: Actually, …

Once you've noticed the story you are telling, say, "I'm telling myself _____. Actually, _____." After "actually," fill in the details that weren't a part of your story. For example, you were frustrated because you had a fight with your friend, and were telling yourself that she doesn't like you anymore. Your "actually" might be "actually, she's been really sad about her parents' divorce and that might be why she's acting so upset." *Actually* is a chance to see the situation clearly, or from a new perspective.

W: Wise action

Once you've identified how you are feeling, the story you are telling, and what is actually happening, you are in a much better position to make a wise choice. Using the example above, you might decide that the wise action is to apologize to your friend and ask if there is anything you can do to help her. Or you might decide that the wise action is to ask your parents for help. Or maybe the wise action is to simply wait and let your emotions settle. There's not necessarily a "right" action that must be taken; wise action means acting based on observation and reflection, not only based on your initial emotions and judgments.

REWIND

Even with all the breathing and soothing and noticing that we can do, we will sometimes make unwise choices and react in an unskillful way. Our children will, too. And while we can impose consequences for inappropriate behavior, it's extremely important to give children the opportunity to reflect when they didn't make a wise choice.

YOU WILL NEED

A time when your child is in a calm state and able to reflect on a recent time when she made an unwise choice

TRY THIS TOGETHER

Ensure that your child knows that this activity/conversation is about learning from mistakes, and is not about judgment or punishment. As best you can, try to refrain from injecting your interpretations about what happened and support your child in processing this difficult moment.

Begin by reminding your child about how our thoughts are a bit like a TV show. Say something like, "Remember how we could use our remote and pause or record the thoughts? Well, today we're going to imagine that we can press the rewind button on a time when we didn't act the way we know we should have. Even though we can't change what happened, we can look back on the situation, play it back slowly, and see how it might have turned out differently."

Ask your child to think of a time in the last week or so (it's best to do this with a relatively fresh memory) when she acted in a way that she now knows she shouldn't have. Maybe it was yelling at a sibling, or an argument with a friend, or a moment of disrespect or backtalk with you. Ask her to close her eyes and remember the day... What was she wearing? What was the weather like that day?

As she recalls this memory, ask if she can remember the beginning of the day. Did she wake up feeling rested, or was she tired? Leading up to the "incident," what was her day like? Was she having a good day or a bad day? What kind of mood was she in?

Then ask her to imagine that she is getting closer to the time of the day when this incident occurred. What was happening? What does she think "set her off" or triggered her into getting upset or frustrated?

As she was starting to get upset, what started happening in her body? Was her body tight or relaxed? Was her heart beating fast or slow? What thoughts or emotions were present? What was her reaction to these thoughts and sensations? Was she feeling uncomfortable? What actions did she want to take?

Now we're right at the moment when your child acted inappropriately. What, if anything, does she remember from that moment? Does she remember making a choice about her behavior?

Ask your child to briefly remember the behavior—actions taken, words spoken. After she acted in this way, what happened next? How did she feel? What sensations or thoughts or emotions were present? How did the other person react? Can she remember their facial expression, actions, or words?

You might want to point out to your child, especially if her behavior was driven by anger, that sometimes, in the moment, lashing out in anger can feel "good." She might have finally felt heard, or been able to release the nervous system energy that had been building up in her body. If your child indicates this, refrain from judging it or telling her that it is "wrong" to feel that way.

Ask your child what happened in the few hours and days after this incident. If the initial outburst felt good, did it still feel good a few hours later? Did she talk to the person afterward about what happened? Did this other person ever tell her how they felt?

Your child may need a short rest or break (maybe a minute of mindful breathing) before moving into the second step of the "Rewind" exercise. Ask your child to imagine that this was a TV show that she was watching a recording of. As she was watching the beginning, could she have predicted what was going to happen? (For example, if she woke up feeling tired and cranky, and had a hard day at school, she might realize that she was a bit "primed" for a difficult encounter later in the day.) See if she can identify the choice points in this incident: when during the day or the actual event could she have made a different choice in her behavior? What might have been a wiser action to take? Did she apologize for her behavior or attempt to reconcile with the other person? (Again, remind your child this is not about blame or shame, it's about learning from mistakes!)

Finally, ask your child, based on what she has reviewed about the situation, what would she do differently next time? What other choices could she have made?

VARIATIONS FOR AGES 3-6

• For younger children, it's best to do this when the event is still fresh in their mind (either later that day or perhaps the next day). Otherwise, it may be too difficult for them to work with a relatively accurate memory of the event.

• Ask your child to illustrate the event, drawing a few different pictures: how she felt that day, what made her upset, how she reacted, and how she felt afterward. Ask your child to explain each of the pictures to you as a springboard for a conversation about how the scene could have played out differently.

• Reflecting on all the techniques she's tried so far, your child can create another illustration depicting how mindfulness could have helped her handle the situation more skillfully.

VARIATIONS FOR AGES 7-11

• Your older child can create a more detailed illustrated timeline of the event, documenting how she felt prior to the incident, the thoughts she had as she was getting triggered, the emotions she noticed, and why she ultimately chose the behavior she did. See if she can indicate the various "choice points" on her timeline: where could she have resourced herself better? When did she have a choice to handle things differently?

• Ask your child to create a new timeline, showing how she could have brought the mindfulness strategies she has learned to this situation, and how she would have handled it differently.

More to Explore

An important part of this activity is understanding that if we are not fully resourced (with sleep, nutrition, time to relax, etc.), we are more likely to act in ways that are unskillful. Most children, when doing this activity, realize that they were already tired or stressed out or hungry or something else when their behavior occurred. Take some time to talk to your child about the things that resource them. Do some changes need to occur in her daily routine? Brainstorm ways to make sure that your child is able to be in a state that helps her make wise choices! (This might include practicing the relaxation and attention activities from previous chapters, going to bed a bit earlier, having healthy snacks available when she needs them, or creating a signal word or phrase she can tell you if she realizes she is getting triggered and needs some support.)

CHAPTER 6

APPRECIATE *Cultivating Gratitude and Joy*

As we've seen, mindfulness helps our children develop greater capacities for attention, emotional awareness, and self-regulation during moments of difficulty. It can also help them to bring deliberate attention to their positive experiences so that they may cultivate greater joy and emotional wellbeing.

A lot of research has been conducted in the last few decades in the field of positive psychology. For much of its history, the study of psychology focused on the disorders of the human mind and the causes of mental disequilibrium. Positive psychology, on the other hand, seeks to identify the sources of human flourishing. It is sometimes colloquially referred to as "the science of happiness."

One of the most intriguing findings in the science of happiness is that a large portion of our individual happiness is within our control. Specifically, researchers believe that about 40 percent of our happiness is derived from our intentional behaviors, attitudes, and lifestyle choices (the rest is determined by a combination of genetic factors and life circumstances). These intentional behaviors can be the ways we manage stress or respond to difficult emotions (like the practices described in chapters 1–5), or they can be deliberate strategies to cultivate positive emotions and experiences. These include practices like being grateful, savoring joyful moments, and developing strong social connections.

Most happiness researchers recommend mindfulness as one of the strategies that promote joyful living. In fact, mindfulness is a fundamental prerequisite for the behaviors that lead to greater happiness: we cannot practice gratitude without noticing the things we have right now, and we cannot truly experience a moment of peace or contentment if we are not present for it! (A well-known 2011 study found that people are happiest when they are focused on the present moment; researchers Gilbert and Killingsworth concluded that "a wandering mind is an unhappy mind.")

In this chapter, you'll learn practices based in positive psychology and the "science of happiness" that will encourage your child to savor their positive experiences and build resilience. The previous chapters outlined emergency or "triage" strategies for managing crises, but you can think of the activities that follow as long-term emotional maintenance and preventative care! Therefore, many of the activities do not have an "In the Moment" suggestion. Additionally, some of the exercises are more suitable to older children, so use your best judgment to determine which ones will be most appropriate or understandable for your younger child.

GRATITUDE PRACTICE

There is perhaps no simpler practice for joy than gratitude. Multiple studies have confirmed that people who practice gratitude are happier and more resilient than those who don't. The Buddha said that the mind takes the shape of that upon which it rests; when we direct our attention to the good, we feel good!

TRY THIS TOGETHER

Ask your child what "gratitude" means to him. What does it mean to be thankful or grateful? (He may give a variety of answers; you can help him understand that being grateful means we appreciate what we have, instead of focusing on the things we don't have.)

Ask your child to close his eyes and think about someone or something that he is thankful for (perhaps a family member, a pet, or a friend, or something like his bed or a favorite stuffed animal or blanket). Encourage him to visualize this person or thing: "Imagine this person is with you right now, smiling at you or hugging you. Or imagine that your teddy bear or blanket is right here for you to snuggle. Think about how this person or thing makes you feel. What do you notice in your body? In your face? Your stomach? Your heart? Notice if you feel calm, or peaceful, or happy, or something else?"

IN THE MOMENT

Gratitude can be challenging during difficult times, but it can also be our saving grace in those moments! Encourage your child to appreciate the power of AND. During a difficult phase or experience, we can acknowledge, "It is like this right now, AND…." For example, it might be "I'm sad right now, AND I have my mom and my blanket to help me feel better." This doesn't mean that we should ignore the hardships we face, or that we should "just think positive thoughts." It's simply a recognition that even when things are hard, there's still something to appreciate. The word is deliberately 'And,' not 'But,' because we are embracing the more difficult part, not dismissing it.

After a moment, invite your child to share with you how it felt to really spend time thinking about something or someone he is grateful for. If he felt good, you can point out how little time that took!

Share with your child that some scientists say we need to spend about 10 to 30 seconds thinking about something that is good in order for the good feelings to really sink in. Does 10 or 30 seconds sound like a long time or a short time?

It may seem like a short time, but usually we don't spend that much time thinking about our teddy bear or our grandma and how good they make us feel. Ask your child to choose something or someone else he is thankful for. (You should choose something, too!) Set a timer for 30 seconds, and tell him to spend that time thinking about the person or object, and why it is so important to him.

After 30 seconds, talk about what you both noticed. Did that feel long or short? What did it feel like? What would it be like if we did something like this 5 times a day? 10 times a day?

VARIATION FOR AGES 3-6

• Ask your child to draw a picture of five things or people that he is thankful for. Hang the picture in his bedroom or on the refrigerator, and make a point of taking 30 seconds each day to look at the drawing and think about why those people or things are so important.

VARIATIONS FOR AGES 7-11

• Talk to your child about why gratitude can be considered a mindfulness practice. Do we need to be fully present to be grateful? Does he think we sometimes miss seeing the things that are good in our life when we're not paying attention?

• Using a simple notebook, help your child start a daily gratitude journal, writing down three things each day that he is thankful for. Encourage him to look for both big and little things to appreciate.

More to Explore

• Create a family "gratitude jar." Keep small pieces of paper and a pencil next to it, and anytime someone is grateful for something or someone, they write it down and put it in the jar. Once a week, sit down as a family and review all the things (big and small) that your family is thankful for. You could also invite each person in the family to give an appreciation out loud for something that someone else did for them during the week.

• Incorporate gratitude into your family routines. Encourage everyone to share one thing they are thankful for at dinner each night, or do this as part of your bedtime routine.

• After taking time to practice gratitude, many children start to think about the things that they have that others don't (like a hot meal at night or a roof over their head). You could brainstorm with your child ways that he could help people that don't have what he has.

CATCHING JOY

Humans have what psychologists call a "negativity bias," which predisposes us to focus on negative events and threats, and often causes us to pay less attention to positive or neutral experiences. "Catching joy" is a way to deliberately bring attention to the moments when we experience joy.

TRY THIS TOGETHER

Children often quite naturally experience joyful states: moments of play, rest, connection, engagement, or wonder. We don't need to do anything to manufacture these states; instead, it's important that we notice them and then make them noticeable to our children.

When you notice that your child is joyful—smiling, laughing, connecting with a friend, or absorbed in imaginative or creative play or something that interests him—take a moment to "catch joy" and say something like, "You seem really happy right now. What does that feel like?"

YOU WILL NEED

Your powers of observation

Encourage your child to notice what he feels in his body when he is happy. Neuroscientist Rick Hanson says that a key to savoring joyful states is to be fully embodied as we are experiencing them. In this practice, you are helping your child turn these positive, happy moments into a more lasting joyful state. The more your child is aware of what happiness feels like, and when he experiences happiness, the more he will cultivate joy.

VARIATION FOR AGES 3-6

• Since "joy" can be an abstract concept for younger children, it will help to coach your child in noticing what the moment feels like. You could ask questions like, "Are you smiling? Does your belly or heart feel warm? Does your body feel light?" These more concrete questions will help your child connect more fully to the abstract notion of joy.

VARIATION FOR AGES 7-11

• Older children might be interested in exploring the brain's negativity bias a bit further. At the end of the day, ask your child to recall 5 or 10 significant things that happened to him. See if the events he recounts are more likely to be positive or negative. If they are negative, encourage your child to look for the positive, joyful events in his day, too. Ask if he thinks an equal number of positive events also happened.

More to Explore

• Create a "Joy Journal." Each day, encourage your child to write down, or draw a picture of, one thing that brought him joy. Ask him to show in the drawing or describe what he felt in his body. How did he know he was happy?

• Ask your child to be *your* joy catcher! When does he notice *you* happy and relaxed and peaceful?

"I'M BORED!"

Parents often dread hearing "I'm bored" from their child. But boredom doesn't have to be a problem; in fact, helping our children learn to tolerate boredom, and unlock its many gifts, is an essential task of parenting. The next time your child tells you that he is bored, encourage him to be mindful of his boredom.

TRY THIS TOGETHER

When your child tells you that he is bored, ask, "What does boredom feel like?"

You'll likely get an initial response like "bad" or "boring." Encourage your child to notice what he feels in his body. Perhaps there is restlessness, energy, hunger, anger, tiredness, relaxation, contentment, or something else. See if he can notice these sensations for a few moments, and see if they change. If he pays attention to boredom, is he still bored?

Ask your child if there is anything good about boredom. What would happen if he let his mind wander for a little bit? (Although daydreaming technically is not a form of mindfulness, it is an important mental state that gives rise to creativity and imagination. Perhaps guide your child in a mind-wandering exercise, just noticing where his thoughts go… the wilder, the better!)

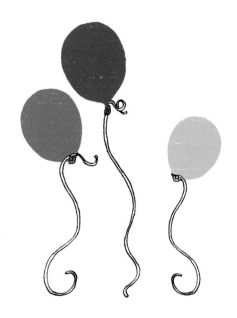

In our increasingly busy and over-scheduled days, children sometimes label downtime or non-activity as "boredom." If your child's responses when you asked him about what boredom felt like in his body indicated a relaxed, at-ease state, you could gently guide him into a conversation about the benefits and pleasant sensations of boredom and stillness. For example, you could ask him:

• What does it feel like when you don't have to concentrate on something?

• Do you think you notice more when you're not actually focused on something? (For example, noticing the sounds in the room or the view out their bedroom window.)

• Do you think boredom could be a chance to let your body rest for a few moments? How often do you think you rest and take breaks during the day?

It might also be helpful for you to share from your own experience what it is like to have downtime, when you don't have to do anything in particular, and when you don't have to take in information or respond to the outside world (as rare as those moments may be!).

VARIATION FOR AGES 3-6

• Though all children are different, you may have a young child that is constantly on the go—it's not so much that boredom is the problem, it's that he doesn't stop! If that's the case, try "catching relaxation" the same way you practiced catching joy—point out to your child the times when he is still and relaxed, and ask him what it feels like.

VARIATIONS FOR AGES 7-11

• With an older child, you could use a car analogy to explore boredom: we often drive our car in just one of two gears—forward and reverse. But there is also neutral. Is boredom a negative, unpleasant feeling, or is it just neutral? Why do we often interpret "neutral" as unpleasant?

• Ask your child if he thinks he turns to the TV or other devices when he is bored. Can he try to be more mindful of when he is using technology? When he turns to his device, is he looking for something specific, or is it because he doesn't know what else to do? The next time he feels bored and starts to reach for a screen, can he try something low-tech instead, and notice how that feels? It might help to brainstorm with your child a list of screen-free activities that he enjoys that he could do when he's feeling bored.

WHAT MAKES ME HAPPY

In this activity, your child will be a "happiness detective," looking for the things that make him happy and create joy. This is a great activity for children of all ages.

TRY THIS TOGETHER

If you've already explained the negativity bias (see page 95) to your child, you can remind him that we often focus on the things that frustrate or upset us, and we sometimes ignore the things that make us feel happy or content.

    Ask your child to create a list (either writing or drawing) of the things that make him happy. Create two columns: one for things that create short-term happiness (like eating donuts), and the other for things that bring longer-lasting happiness (like spending time with family). Encourage him to think of activities he likes to do, objects that make him happy (like a comfort

YOU WILL NEED

Paper and pens/crayons/markers

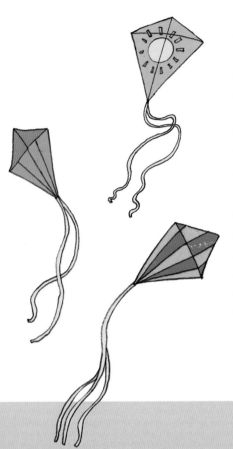

blanket or a favorite toy, for example), people he likes to be with, or thoughts that bring joy. Explain that there are lots of things that can make us happy, and it doesn't matter if it's something quite little or something very important.

As your child makes his list, talk to him about the things he chose and how they make them feel. What does he think it means to be happy? Why is it important to know what makes us happy?

When your child has finished his list, post it in his room or somewhere he can see it. It's a powerful reminder of things he can be grateful for, AND it can be a helpful resource for him when he is feeling bored, or when he needs to be cheered up. It's very empowering for children to recognize the things that they can do for themselves in order to resource themselves emotionally.

More to Explore

Encourage your child to make another list, this time identifying the things he can do to make other people happy. Have him consider the big and small acts of kindness he could engage in:

• Offering a sincere compliment

• Holding the door open for someone

• Coloring a picture for someone, making them a card, or writing them a note

• Inviting someone to play with him

• Giving a hug

Can he do one thing on that list each week?

MINDFUL EATING

Mindful eating is a beautiful practice that incorporates gratitude, savoring joy, and understanding our connection to the larger world.

TRY THIS TOGETHER

Remind your child that mindfulness is a way of paying attention… and we can pay attention to anything, including eating! Ask if he sometimes eats unmindfully, without really noticing how his food looks or even tastes. With mindful eating, we will bring our close attention to something we do many times a day, without really being aware of it.

Hand your child the snack that you will be eating. First ask him to just look at it. What does he notice? If he had never seen this food before, how would he describe it (shape, size, color)? Does he notice anything that he hasn't really ever seen, even though he's eaten this food before?

Now smell the food. What does it smell like? Encourage your child to be really specific in his description. If he says that chocolate smells "sweet," ask him what sweet smells like. Does he notice that he's getting hungry or that his mouth is salivating as he starts to look at and smell the food?

How does the food feel? Can he feel the ridges in the raisin or the smoothness of the chocolate?

Next, place the food just on the tip of his tongue. What tastes does he notice?

Challenge your child to take a whole minute to eat this snack and chew as slowly as possible. Is there part of him that just wants to swallow it right away? Is there a sense of trying to rush? If so, just notice that and encourage him to keep chewing slowly. What tastes does he notice? (He can share his answers once he's finished eating.) When he swallows, encourage him to notice the sensations of swallowing and the food going into his stomach.

What was it like to eat so slowly? What would it be like if we ate like this all the time?

YOU WILL NEED

A small snack that's easy to eat slowly, such as raisins or a piece of chocolate.

More to Explore

• You could try starting a new family ritual where you spend the first minute of a meal in silence, so you can truly taste the food.

• If you're in the habit of eating with the TV on or with your gadgets on the table, try removing all distractions. How did this change the experience of eating a meal?

APPRECIATING OUR FOOD

As a follow-up to the mindful eating practice, you can use this activity to help your child fully appreciate his food and all that went into preparing it.

YOU WILL NEED

Time to go to the grocery store together and cook a meal together

TRY THIS TOGETHER

Talk to your child about what mindful eating was like, and ask him to imagine what it would be like if he ate an entire meal mindfully. Is that how he normally eats? (You could talk about how we often eat with lots of distractions around us —phones or TVs—or we often eat on-the-go, rushing through our meal to get to the next activity.) What would it be like if we slowed down, just for right now, the process of getting and making and acquiring our food?

Invite your child to look through a recipe book with you to pick out a meal he'd like to try, or decide on a favorite family meal to prepare. Make a list together of all the ingredients that you will need… and head to the store!

As you shop, use your mindful seeing and listening and smelling to notice as much as you can at the supermarket. Notice the smells from the fruit aisle and from the bakery and from the coffee shop… Do they make you feel hungry?

Encourage your child to notice the colors and textures of the foods and ingredients that you purchase. Depending on your child's age, let him push the cart and select items from the shelves so that his entire body is involved in the process of gathering your food.

When it's time to make the meal, involve your child as much as it is appropriate for him: he can sort the groceries, measure ingredients, or rinse or chop or stir. As he does this, encourage him to notice what his body is doing, and to be aware of the sights and smells of the food. It will help for you to bring your "beginner's mind" to this activity, too, imagining you were seeing these foods for the same time. I remember the first time I made dinner with my daughter, she was absolutely fascinated by all the layers of an onion!

Use your mindful eating practices from the activity above as you eat your meal. Savor each bite as you think about all that went into acquiring and preparing the food. Can you taste each of the ingredients that were used? Do you notice more when you eat slowly? Do you feel any differently when you eat slowly? (Some children may notice that they feel "full" sooner, or that they tasted things more.)

At the end of the meal, take a moment to express gratitude for all the people that contributed to it, from the farmers and grocery-store workers to the people who cooked it. As you clean up, continue to be mindful as you wash the dishes and appreciate yummy food and a loving family to share it with.

More to Explore

Before a meal, take a few moments to think about where your food came from. Who grew the vegetables? Who raised the chicken? Who baked the bread? How much sunlight and energy were used to bring this food to your plate? How did the food get to the grocery store? Who displayed the food and kept it fresh? How did the meal get made? Express your gratitude for all the people, animals, forms of energy, and parts of the earth that went into your meal.

CHAPTER 7

CONNECT *Nurturing Empathy and Relationships*

In this chapter, our exploration of mindfulness comes full circle. We began in Chapter 1 with ourselves, discovering how to soothe our frazzled nervous systems and be fully present with our children. You learned how to be a stable, nurturing anchor for your child as she learned how to calm her own states of overwhelm and frustration. Gradually, she's learned to expand her attention outward, from inner sensations, thoughts, and emotions to the joyful experiences all around her. Ultimately, mindfulness practice helps us see our connections to the larger social and environmental networks around us, and we discover how our interactions with others and with the natural world can be a further support for our individual states of concentration and calm.

The more we pay attention to the world around us, the more we realize the interconnected nature of all things. Our nervous systems impact the nervous systems of those around us. Our actions leave an imprint on our environment, on a local and global level. Our words profoundly influence the emotions and thoughts of others.

Our health depends on the health and safety of the food and water on our planet. We are social creatures, and we live in an interconnected web of relationships with other people, without whom we literally would not survive.

As your child grows older, her social world of friendships becomes more important. As you likely know from your own experience, our relationships are an incredible source of joy, but can also be where we experience our greatest stress and wounding. Maintaining healthy relationships is an important life skill, and just like paying attention or calming down, it is a skill we don't often explicitly teach our children. In this chapter, we'll explore how mindfulness can help children nurture their relationships with friends and family, through developing empathy and communication skills. It includes activities that nurture your child's sense of connection to others and the larger world by exploring her connections to her community and the environment.

JUST LIKE ME

This is an empathy-building activity to help your child understand that even the kids they don't get along with, even those who are mean to them, are in many ways just like them.

TRY THIS TOGETHER

Ask your child to think of a good friend and identify all the things that they have in common. Talk about how we are usually drawn to people who are similar to us and have similar interests. We may sometimes think that the people who aren't our friends, or who we disagree with, are very different from us, but in many ways, they are just like us.

Ask your child to close her eyes and take a few deep breaths, or do a different mindfulness practice that helps her feel calm. Next, ask her to think of a person that she thinks she is very different from, or doesn't have a lot in common with. It could also be someone she doesn't get along with. Tell your child that you are going to say a series of statements about this person, and you want her to silently repeat each of the statements in her own mind. Here are some examples:

"Just like me, this person is a human being, with a mind and a body and thoughts and feelings."

"Just like me, this person wants to laugh and play and have fun."

"Just like me, this person sometimes feels sad and lonely."

"Just like me, this person feels bad when they are left out."

"Just like me, this person sometimes makes mistakes."

"Just like me, this person sometimes gets angry, and says things they don't mean."

"Just like me, this person wants to be happy."

"Just like me, this person sometimes feels embarrassed."

"Just like me, this person wants to be accepted for who they are."

"Just like me, this person deserves love and understanding."

IN THE MOMENT

When your child is upset about a conflict with a friend or classmate, start by encouraging her to take a deep breath and use a calming exercise that works well for her. Ask her to notice her emotions, and any thoughts she is having about this person. Then you can remind her of the Just Like Me practice, and suggest some the statements from the practice that would help her put the situation in perspective, or create your own. For example, you could offer, "Just like me, this person gets frustrated with her friends," or "Just like me, this person is doing the best she can."

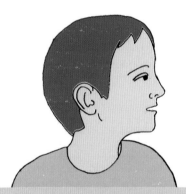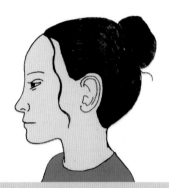

More to Explore

Talk to your older child about what this practice was like for her. Was it easy or hard? Does she feel any differently toward this person now? If so, how? Does she want to perhaps learn a little more about them?

VARIATION FOR AGES 3-6

• Ask your younger child if any of the "just like me" phrases were surprising to her. (Perhaps she hadn't really thought before about how other children also feel bad when they are left out, or just want to be accepted, too.) Can she now name a few things that she and this person have in common?

I HEAR YOU

You may have already done mindful listening exercises with your child (see page 51). In this activity, you'll help your child understand what it feels like to be completely listened to. Then you'll help your child practice listening carefully to what another person is saying. This activity is good for children of all ages.

YOU WILL NEED

A phone or timer

TRY THIS TOGETHER

Ask your child if she ever notices that during a conversation, she is sometimes thinking more about what she is going to say next than listening to what the person is actually saying. Or if she ever gets interrupted when she is talking? Or if she feels like the other person doesn't really "get" what she's saying? Explain that we can be mindful when we're talking to people so we can better understand them and communicate more effectively.

For this exercise, you and your child will each take turns speaking while the other person listens with their full attention. Choose a topic that you each can share your perspective on— perhaps a minor disagreement that you had recently, or a time when your child became upset. For younger children, you could each state your opinion on a "controversy": Is pizza better than a sandwich? Ask your child to tell you her side of the story (her opinion, how she saw the events unfolding, how she was feeling, etc.). Depending on your child's age (less time for younger children), set a timer for 2-3 minutes and then allow her to speak… and you don't get to say anything! All you are going to do is listen (this can be a great mindfulness practice for you, too!). You are giving your child a chance to be completely heard.

When your child finishes, if you think it would be helpful you can paraphrase or summarize what she said, and ask if you understood her correctly. If you did not, offer her another opportunity to share her point of view. Thank your child for sharing her thoughts with you.

Now you describe your perspective—and your child listens. Set the timer, and when you are done, depending on your child's age, she can summarize what you said. Then take a few moments to talk about what this experience was like:

- What was it like to be listened to without being interrupted? How did it feel?

- How did it feel to listen to someone without interrupting? Did you want to say something? Did you find yourself wanting to defend yourself, or getting upset, or something else?

- What would it be like if we always listened this carefully to other people?

- Do you think the other person understood you better after this exercise?

- Do you think you understood the other person better?

IN THE MOMENT

When you are arguing with your child, consider setting a timer and allowing each person to calmly state their observations or perspective. If possible, sit somewhere you can feel calm (maybe even take a brief time-out first). Set ground rules (no name-calling, describe things as objectively as possible, without making judgments). This is a challenging skill for young people, so it's important for you to model to your child how to state observations instead of judgments (e.g., "Your toys are in the hallway instead of your room" instead of "You're so messy leaving your toys in the hallway.") When it's your child's turn to speak, do your best to listen, giving her the space to say what has upset her and how she feels. Resist the urge to defend yourself and simply listen to her experience and perspective.

More to Explore

Incorporate mindful listening into your family dinners once a week. Allow each person 2 minutes to speak, with no interruptions. They can share anything they want to, and enjoy the experience of being fully listened to. After everyone has had a turn, each person can share an appreciation for something another person said, or identify something new or interesting they learned by listening carefully.

FRIENDSHIP PRACTICE: FEELINGS AND NEEDS

This is a powerful practice to share with your child if she is having a difficult time with a friend. The following exercise is based on the principles of Nonviolent Communication (NVC), developed by Marshall Rosenberg. You can learn more about NVC, and download free resources, at www.cnvc.org.

YOU WILL NEED

Visit www.cnvc.org to download a comprehensive list of feelings and needs

TRY THIS TOGETHER

In short, Nonviolent Communication is based on the principle that we behave in a certain way in order to meet a need. When we are upset with someone, it's likely that they are engaging in a behavior that does not meet our needs, or impairs our ability to meet our needs. If we can identify our feelings about the situation, whether it's frustration, anger, resentment, jealousy, sadness, or something else, we can discover the unmet needs that are generating these feelings. We can then communicate to this person how we are feeling, and what we need. This is a radically different way of working out differences—instead of blaming the other person, in NVC we take responsibility for our feelings and speak of our own needs. We try to reach a solution that can meet everyone's needs.

Ask your child to tell you (if she hasn't already) about the conflict or difficulty that she is having with her friend. While friendship difficulties can take many different forms, it's likely that it can be simplified into a story of someone acting, or speaking, in a way we do not want them to. We may be mad at how someone has treated us, or we are wishing someone would act differently.

As your child considers this difficulty or conflict, ask her to think about a recent specific incident with this person where they did something that your child did not want them to do (or they didn't do something they did want them to do). Once your child identifies this, ask, "What did you want your friend to do instead?".

And then ask, "Why? Why did you want them to do that?".

At this point, you will likely get an answer that's superficial, or at best incomplete. Keep asking your child "Why?" until you reach a deeper answer that hints at your child's unmet need. You can ask questions like, "Why would that matter to you?" "What is important to you about that?" "What would you get if they acted this way?"

(For example, if your child is frustrated with a classmate who isn't following all the rules of a game they play, your child may first say that they just want this person to follow the rules! Why? Because those are the rules! Why? Well, it's not fun/not fair if they don't follow the rules. Why? Because then everyone else argues and we just waste our playtime fighting instead of having fun. Now you've gotten to some real emotions (anger, frustration) and needs (fairness, fun, belonging).

Depending on the situation, help your child to identify what really matters to her about this conflict. Help her understand what she needs (to have fun, to play, to know that the game is fair).

Ask your child, "Why do you think this person doesn't follow the rules? What do they get by not following the rules?"

At first, it may be hard for your child to see the situation from the other child's perspective, or she may respond by blaming or judging, with statements like "Because he's mean." "Because he doesn't like me." As you did earlier, keep asking "Why?" until you can get to a deeper human need that may be beneath the not-following-the-rules behavior (for example, this other child may have a need to be heard, to understand, to contribute their own ideas, etc.). Your child might realize

that this other child has many of the same underlying needs they do! Not following the rules of their game is a strategy this other child is using to try to meet their needs. How could they find a way to meet everyone's needs?

Next, help your child brainstorm a way that she could explain her feelings and needs to this other person in a way that avoids judgment and blame. The general formula for doing this in NVC is to say, "When {this behavior} happens, I feel {emotion} because I need {underlying need}/because it's important to me that {need}." For example, "When you skipped my turn yesterday, I felt frustrated because it's important to me that things are fair and fun, and that I get to be a part of the game with everyone." In this way, your child states her feelings and needs in a way that takes ownership for her emotions, but also allows the other child to realize he or she may have the same needs, too. They invite this person to see things from their perspective.

Finally, your child can make a request: "Would you be able to let everyone take their turns in order if we agree to change the order we go in every week?" Or offer a different solution that could meet both of their needs.

Nonviolent Communication is a powerful skill to develop, and it's hard to do it justice in one short lesson, but exercises like these in which you encourage your child to understand her own feelings and needs, as well as those of others, and help her brainstorm solutions that honor everyone's needs can go a long way to more peaceful conflict resolution.

IN THE MOMENT

When you are in the middle of a difficult moment with your child, take a deep breath and ask, with sincerity, "What do you need?" She may not know what she needs, but it's a powerful question to ask. Accepting the premise that all behaviors are done in order to meet a need, can you guess what the underlying need for your child's tantrum or outburst is? Does she need security, or predictability, or something to eat? Use some of the calming strategies from Chapter 2 and then see if you and your child can get to the bottom of what's bothering her.

VARIATIONS FOR AGES 3–6

• The NVC activity may be too difficult for younger children, but it's never too early to start helping children develop their emotional vocabulary (see Chapter 4) or identify the important needs that are beneath their behaviors. You can help your child understand this by narrating what you observe: "You are crying and came over to me for a hug. I'm wondering if you are scared, and need to feel safe?"

• You can make similar observations and ask questions about other situations. For example, when reading a book, you could say, "The girl's mom was really upset when she came home all dirty and messy. I wonder how the mom was feeling? What do you think she needed?"

VARIATIONS FOR AGES 7–11

• Print out the lists of human needs from www.cnvc.org. Discuss the needs with your child and ask her to identify which are most important to her. How does she feel when those needs aren't met?

• Encourage your child to practice seeing her experiences through this lens of feelings and needs. How does she feel when her needs are met? What strategies does she use to meet her needs? Can she see the behavior of others as a way to meet their underlying needs?

NOTICING WALK

In this activity, you and your children will explore your connections to your neighborhood and your immediate environment. You'll exercise your powers of observation, and also reflect on the ways that you impact the world around you and how you can care for it.

YOU WILL NEED

A nice day to take a walk in your neighborhood. If you'd like, bring a plastic bag and some gloves so you can pick up any trash you find.

TRY THIS TOGETHER

On your "noticing walk," the goal is to notice as many things about your neighborhood as possible, especially things that you may have never paid attention to before. You might want to encourage your child to be silent during the walk, or if that is too much of a challenge, you could walk for two minutes in silence, share what you see, and then repeat.

Encourage your child to notice things like the details on the houses, how many trees are in each yard, the signs, flowers, and animals she sees, things she can smell, the sounds she can hear, and if she can feel wind or sunlight on her skin. Invite her to use all of her senses as she takes in the world around her. How many living things does she encounter?

If you do this walk throughout the year, talk about the changes that you can notice—different animals that you encounter, trees sprouting or dropping their leaves, neighbors changing things about their houses. This is a gentle way of reminding your children that things are always changing around us, but we sometimes don't notice it unless we look carefully.

Ask your child how her activity also impacts and changes the neighborhood—the footprints she leaves, the trash she picks up, the oxygen she breathes in, the carbon dioxide she breathes out, the people she says hi to, the flowers she plants. How do we impact the environment, and how does it impact us?

If she notices trash along the walk, encourage her to pick it up if she has gloves. You might wonder aloud how the trash we leave behind might impact the animals in the area.

VARIATION FOR AGES 3-6

• Draw pictures after your walk, and compare them to previous walks to see how much things change.

VARIATIONS FOR AGES 7-11

• List 10 things you could do to help keep your neighborhood clean and safe.

• Research who the original inhabitants of your neighborhood were, and consider how much things have changed since then.

More to Explore

When you get home, talk about what you noticed. Do you feel more connected to your neighborhood when you pay closer attention to it? If you've done several of these walks, talk about the changes you have noticed.

LOVINGKINDNESS

Mindfulness is more than just paying attention; it is paying attention with kindness. We support the cultivation of a kind attitude, and kind actions, through the practice of lovingkindness. Our mind is said to take the shape of what it rests on, and this sweet practice nurtures the heart by deliberately generating and expressing kind thoughts for others, and for ourselves.

TRY THIS TOGETHER

Read the following script to your child:

Close your eyes, relax your body, and take a few deep breaths…

Take a moment to think about a time when someone did something kind for you. Maybe someone gave you a special gift, or maybe they helped you when you were sad or frustrated… As you think about this kind act that someone did for you, take a moment to notice how it felt. What was it like to receive kindness? How did you feel? Even thinking about it now, what do you notice in your body—in your chest, your stomach, your face?

For most of us, kindness—receiving it, and giving it—feels really good. Today we are going to practice sending kindness to another person, so take a moment and think about someone who is really important to you that you would like to send some kindness to…

Picture this person in your mind… See their face… Imagine they are right here in front of you, smiling at you…

We're going to send some kind wishes to this person. In just a moment, I will say a short phrase, and then you can silently repeat the words in your head, imagining that you are saying them to this special person…

I wish for you to be happy…

I wish for you to be safe and healthy and strong…

I wish for you to feel peaceful…

I wish for you to be loved…

Take another deep breath, and notice what it felt like to send these kind wishes to this important person…

Now, I'm going to repeat the phrases, but this time, you are going to send the wishes to yourself!
I wish to be happy…
I wish to be safe and healthy and strong…
I wish to feel peaceful…
I wish to be loved…
I deserve to be happy, safe, peaceful, and loved.
Take another deep breath, and notice how it feels to send kind thoughts to yourself.
Notice any sensations you feel in your body, or any feelings that are present.

VARIATION FOR AGES 3-6

• You may want to do this as two separate practices—once sending kind thoughts to another person, and another time asking your child to send the thoughts to herself. For younger children, it's often easier to start by sending the thoughts to themselves, and then offering them to someone else.

VARIATION FOR AGES 7-11

• Encourage your child to come up with their own special phrases for sending kind thoughts to themselves and others.

More to Explore

Write, or draw, your kind wishes for someone in a letter, and send it to them! How does it feel to send it? Once they receive the letter, ask the person how they felt. How does it feel to bring happiness to others?

INTENTIONAL ACTS OF KINDNESS

While random acts of kindness are always welcomed, intentional acts of kindness are a wonderful way to engage with the world. In this activity, you and your child can brainstorm all the ways you can bring kindness to others. This is a great activity for children of all ages.

TRY THIS TOGETHER

YOU WILL NEED

• Paper and crayons/markers/pens

• Post-it notes

• Poster board

Remind your child about how it feels good when we receive kindness from other people. Can she think of a time when she did something kind for someone? What did that feel like?

Brainstorm all the ways we can show kindness to other people. You could create a sign or poster with the following categories: "Kind Words I Can Say," "Everyday Acts of Kindness," and "Special Kindness Projects." Fill out each list together, and as you do, talk about how those acts would impact people. You can point out how even small acts or words can make a big difference to people's days, and people's lives. Can you do one small act of kindness each day?

Choose one of the bigger "Kindness Projects" to work on together for a few weeks. Perhaps it's organizing a service project, helping out a family member, or volunteering in your community.

Share with your child that researchers have also found that we feel better when we see others do kind things for people. Create another poster to keep at home where you write down the kind acts you witness each day. (You can remind your child about the negativity bias (see page 95), which leads us to pay more attention to negative events, and tell her that it can also mean we pay more attention to the unkind acts we see each day.) How many kind acts does she think she can see in one day? Use the post-it notes to add to the poster each day as a celebration of kindness.

More to Explore

• If you have a family gratitude practice or ritual at dinner or bedtime each night, add kindness to your practice! Ask everyone to share one kind thing they did, or that was done for them, each day.

• Your older child can keep a kindness journal, documenting kind acts each day.

MINDFUL REMINDERS

BEGIN WITH YOU

The final words I'd like to share with you are the ones with which I opened this book: the most important way you will teach mindfulness, focus, and resilience to your children is by embodying these skills yourself. The place to begin is with YOU. Start your own personal mindfulness practice before sharing mindfulness with your child. You'll understand the concepts in these activities better, and you'll have a wealth of stories and examples from your own practice that you can share with your child. And, you'll likely find that your own patience, concentration, and resilience are strengthened, too.

BE PATIENT

As you'll find in your own practice, the benefits of mindfulness can take time to show up. Be patient with your child, allowing her to learn and absorb what you are teaching her according to her own timeline. If there are times when you feel mindfulness "isn't working," rely on your own practice to check in with your expectations, and to trust that what you are teaching and sharing with your child *is* working. The beauty of parenting is seeing the things you teach to your children blossom in their own time. Mindfulness is a practice, a set of skills you and your child can work on together for many years.

KEEP IT FUN

Your child does a lot of formal and structured learning, so let mindfulness be fun and playful. If your child doesn't like a particular activity, don't force it—try a different activity.

LISTEN TO YOUR CHILD

Ask your child which mindfulness practices seem to be most helpful for her (you can use the checklist opposite). Talk to her about what she notices as she experiments with various mindfulness activities. Remember there is no right or wrong way to react to a mindfulness activity—the point is to notice our experiences. Enjoy this opportunity to learn about your child and her inner world.

I wish you many moments of joyful exploration!

CHECKLIST OF ACTIVITIES

SOOTHE

☐ Belly Breathing (see page 32)
☐ Tension Tamer (see page 34)
☐ Calm Detective (see page 36)
☐ Deep Relaxation (see page 39)
☐ My Safe Place (see page 42)

FOCUS

☐ My Mind in a Jar (see page 46)
☐ Find Your Anchor (see page 48)
☐ Mindful Listening (see page 51)
☐ Mindful Seeing (see page 53)
☐ Oh, Those Distractions! (see page 55)
☐ Attention: Microscope and Telescope
   (see page 57)

FEEL

☐ Emotion Charades (see page 62)
☐ My Amazing Emotions (see page 64)
☐ Reading Emotions (see page 66)
☐ A Text from My Brain (see page 68)
☐ Holding My Emotions (see page 69)

PAUSE

☐ Neural Wi-Fi (see page 74)
☐ The TV Show in my Head (see page 77)
☐ Oh, The Stories We Tell! (see page 81)
☐ I Saw (see page 85)
☐ Rewind (see page 86)

APPRECIATE

☐ Gratitude Practice (see page 92)
☐ Catching Joy (see page 95)
☐ "I'm Bored!" (see page 97)
☐ What Makes Me Happy (see page 99)
☐ Mindful Eating (see page 101)
☐ Appreciating our Food (see page 102)

CONNECT

☐ Just Like Me (see page 106)
☐ I Hear You (see page 108)
☐ Friendship Practice: Feelings and Needs
   (see page 110)
☐ Noticing Walk (see page 114)
☐ Lovingkindness (see page 116)
   Intentional Acts of Kindness (see page 118)

MY CHILD'S FAVORITE MINDFUL ACTIVITIES

WHAT I'VE LEARNED ABOUT MY CHILD

RESOURCES

BOOKS
Mindfulness for Parents

Mindful Moments for Busy Mothers: Daily Meditations and Mantras for Greater Calm, Balance, and Joy by Sarah Rudell Beach, CICO Books, 2018

Everyday Blessings: Mindfulness for Parents by Myla and Jon Kabat-Zinn, Piatkus, 2014

Parenting from the Inside Out: How a Deeper Self-Understanding Can Help You Raise Children Who Thrive by Daniel J. Siegel and Mary Hartzell, TarcherPerigee, 2013

Parenting in the Present Moment: How to Stay Focused on What Really Matters by Carla Naumburg, Ph.D., Parallax Press, 2014

The Conscious Parent: Transforming Ourselves, Empowering Our Children by Shefali Tsabary, Ph.D, Yellow Kite Publishing, 2015

Mindfulness for Children

Duck! Rabbit! by Amy Krouse Rosenthal and Tom Lichtenheld, Chronicle Books, 2009

Mindful Games: Sharing Mindfulness and Meditation with Children, Teens, and Families by Susan Kaiser Greenland, Shambhala, 2016

Oh! by Josse Goffin and Harry N. Abrams, RMN, 2003

Planting Seeds: Practicing Mindfulness with Children by Thich Nhat Hanh and the Plum Village Community, Parallax Press, 2011

Ready, Set, Breathe: Practicing Mindfulness with Your Children for Fewer Meltdowns and a More Peaceful Family by Carla Naumburg, Ph.D., New Harbinger Publications, 2016

Sitting Still Like a Frog: Mindful Exercises for Kids (and Their Parents) by Eline Snel, Shambhala, 2014

Teaching Mindfulness Skills to Kids and Teens, edited by Christopher Willard and Amy Saltzman, Guilford Press, 2017

The Whole-Brain Child: 12 Proven Strategies to Nurture Your Child's Developing Mind by Daniel J. Siegel, M.D., and Tina Payne Bryson, Ph.D, Bantam, 2012

WEBSITES

Mindful Schools: www.mindfulschools.org

Left Brain Buddha: leftbrainbuddha.com

The Greater Good Science Center: greatergood.berkeley.edu/

Mindful.org: www.mindful.org

Susan Kaiser Greenland: www.susankaisergreenland.com/

APPS

Stop, Breathe, and Think: https://www.stopbreathethink.com

Smiling Mind: https://www.smilingmind.com.au

VIDEO

Dr Daniel Siegel presenting a hand model of the brain and 'Flip Your Lid": https://www.youtube.com/watch?v=gm9ClJ74Oxw

INDEX

ACKNOWLEDGMENTS

A huge thank you to the team at CICO for their work in seeing this book from conception to delivery. Thank you to Kristine Pidkameny, Dawn Bates, and Cindy Richards for your support, feedback, and commitment. And a special thank you to Rosie Scott for the illustrations that bring warmth and heart to these pages.

I want to thank my teachers who have supported me in my mindfulness practice. I am especially thankful for my colleagues at Mindful Schools, who have inspired me through their work with teachers and with young people, and from whom I have learned so much about sharing this practice with children. I also owe a deep debt of gratitude to the teachers who have welcomed me into their classrooms, and to the parents who have welcomed me into their homes, to teach mindfulness to the young people in their care. Each time I share mindfulness with children I gain deeper insight into the nature of this work. Thank you especially to the many students who have been part of my mindfulness classes: you always challenge me and inspire me to become a better teacher.

Finally, I am so appreciative of my incredible family. Thank you to my parents for teaching me to be compassionate, resilient, and joyful. Todd, thank you for your loving support of my practice and my work, and for the life we have built together. Abby and Liam, thank you for practicing and learning mindfulness right along with me. You were my first mindfulness students, and, of course, my favorites! I treasure your insights and deeply appreciate your enthusiasm and your patience. I love you to the moon and back.